Living in the Innovation Age

LIVING
IN
THE INNOVATION AGE

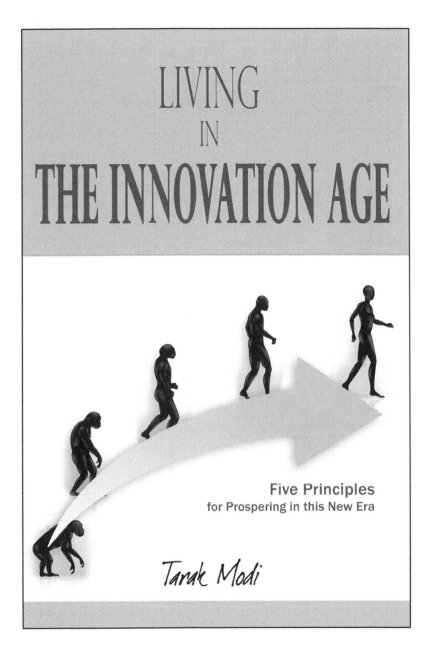

Five Principles
for Prospering in this New Era

Tarak Modi

Library of Congress Cataloging-in-Publication Data
Modi, Tarak.
Living in the Innovation Age: Five Principles for Prospering in this New Era / Modi, Tarak
    p.cm. – (TekNirvana)
ISBN: 0-615-56285-X

ISBN-13: 9780615562858   1. Innovation., 2. Leadership.,3. Executive Ability.
2011937758
http://lccn.loc.gov/2011937758

*To all the sung and unsung heroes
who dedicated themselves in their quest for Innovation.*

Contents

List of Side Boxes

List of Figures

Foreword

I have known and worked closely with Tarak Modi since he joined CALIBRE in the spring of 2010. Since that time, as our Chief Technology Officer, he has energized the innovation process at CALIBRE, and has led our IT strategy development and execution. As the President & Chief Executive Officer of CALIBRE, I believe one of our most vital business strengths is our ability to leverage advances in Information Technology (IT). And a key part of that ability has been, and will always be, our willingness to embrace innovation. Innovation, and the resulting competitive edge it provides, is about providing best-value (efficient and cost-effective) services. It is about driving real performance improvements by not necessarily doing more of the same thing faster and cheaper, but by finding novel ways to solve old problems. Real innovation is about filling a gap that customers may not even know they have. It is about meeting unmet customer needs with solutions that even they might not have envisioned.

As a management and technology services company, CALIBRE has leveraged technology and innovation to sustain our long-term growth and to maintain our strategic competitive advantage. Successful companies must continuously identify, evaluate, and apply innovative, effective, and relevant technologies. When this is accomplished, these companies reap three key benefits:

1. They add even more value for their customers with innovative solutions.
2. They improve their internal business processes to enhance their ability to sell and deliver value-added solutions.
3. They reduce their cost of doing business with increasingly effective and efficient IT-based systems.

Tarak believes that innovation is everyone's job in our globally competitive economy. For innovation to successfully be of real value (and contribute to the bottom line), Tarak shows us that ideas must be followed up with implementation. In Part 1 of his book, *Living in the Innovation Age*, Tarak helps us understand that the ultimate goal of innovation is to create a sustainable competitive advantage. He discusses how, in order to remain competitive, the product or service must provide real value to the consumer, be differentiated from competitors' offerings, and present a significant barrier to imitation.

In Part 2, Tarak introduces five principles that can help organizations prosper in this fundamentally unique era. As he explains, innovation is about creating the future, through visioning and action. I believe successfully applying this concept has driven growth at CALIBRE. In Part 3, Tarak discusses how one can implement innovation in their organization. He presents three techniques that he has applied in his professional career and that have been shown to spur innovation. Finally, in Part 4, Tarak provides an overview of the typical innovation lifecycle from ideation to execution and leaves his readers with a practical, ready-to-use maturity model, which they can use to lead their organizations to their desired stage of innovation maturity.

Throughout his book, Tarak cuts through the status quo of conventional thinking, and walks us through the process that a company must take to innovate and realize its "next big thing." He explains that innovation is not just about introducing something new, it literally means a process that renews something that exists, and effective innovation is more about the implementation of an idea than the idea itself.

Charles Darwin once said that, "It is not the strongest of the species that survive, or the most intelligent, but the one most responsive to change." As Tarak explains, despite creativity and technical expertise, companies fail when they do not embrace innovation and focus on implementation, converting ideas into reality. Innovation is a journey and the road to successful innovation may have struggles along the way; failures are just milestones along this long journey to success. As he further elaborates, living and prospering in this innovation age is neither an option nor a luxury, but an absolute necessity for survival in today's extremely competitive and global economy. In his words, "to survive, business leaders must reevaluate how they think about and approach innovation."

CALIBRE has prospered since 1989 because of its responsiveness and willingness to adapt to changing times. Tarak Modi has spurred the innovation process at CALIBRE. His book clearly explains how one can not only survive but prosper in this fundamentally unique era, the innovation age, in which we now live. Those who read these pages will find their thinking stimulated and their understanding enhanced, as were mine.

I hope you enjoy this book and profit from it.

Joseph A. Martore
President & Chief Executive Officer
CALIBRE Systems, Inc.

Acknowledgements

Writing a book is a journey – not a journey of pages but one of ideas. It is a confluence of thoughts that have been formed, nurtured, and refined over many years with the influence of countless co-workers, friends, and family members. In that respect, the creation of this book is very much like the subject which it covers – Innovation. Just as most innovation is the result of many different hunches that coalesce over time to ultimately result in the "eureka" moment, this book too is much more than just the time it took to put the words on its pages.

I am one of the fortunate ones who has never had a job where they could not learn something new. Much of the credit for that goes to my co-workers over the years for continuously challenging me to be a better professional. CALIBRE has played a pivotal role in my career. I have never seen a company with so many capable and dedicated employees that truly function as one team with one goal. I am truly grateful to Michael Polster for believing in me and making me a part of this wonderful team and for encouraging me at every step of the way to write this book. I am indebted to Jack Mutarelli for helping me understand the importance of getting "traction" and Ted Chopin for always helping me see the practical side of innovation. I owe much to Joe Martore for always keeping me on my toes with his thoughtful questions, deep insight, and business acumen and for agreeing to write the foreword for this book.

I would also like to thank my reviewers for graciously taking time out of their busy schedule to review the draft manuscript as it evolved and help shape it into the book that it is today. I am grateful to Frank Konieczny, Dr. Lynn Lambert, Michael Polster, Jose Ruggero, Rowan Snyder, and Mahesh Paolini-Subramanya for their constructive feedback and valuable insight.

Finally, I am forever indebted to my friends and family for their love and support. Their unwavering belief in me is what kept me going at times when I struggled to put my thoughts into words that made sense. As you might guess, there were several "interesting" moments to say the least, but those are stories for another day and another book!

Introduction

What do you get when a candle maker and a soap maker get together and form a business? Would you believe that together these two would form a company that has not only survived but thrived and prospered for over 175 years? What about a company that began by mining stone from quarries for use in grinding wheels? Could that same company today have over 76,000 employees, 55,000 products, and operations in more than 60 countries?

The first company is Procter & Gamble (P&G). Since their humble beginnings in 1837, P&G has become a Fortune 500 multinational corporation that manufactures a wide range of consumer goods today. They aren't showing any signs of slowing down either. For example, who would have thought of combining their expertise in oral hygiene with their knowledge in cleaning and whitening agents? P&G did exactly that and created Crest Whitestrips®, which makes them over $200M a year. And which company besides P&G would have thought of leveraging a recession along with entrepreneurial people looking for new businesses to start up, consumers seeking affordable luxuries, and a proven cleaning brand to launch a national car wash chain, Mr. Clean Car Wash?

The second company mentioned is 3M. Over the past century 3M also has created a vast array of amazing products that are now household names. For example, any other company would have long discarded an adhesive that did not perform its job of sticking things together and would have recycled its yellow scrap paper; however 3M took those two ingredients and created Post-It notes.

So, why are these companies and others like them so successful, while many others fail and fade away? The simple answer is that somehow the successful companies have mastered the principles of innovation. These

There are *two* appendices at the end of the book:

Appendix A: Innovation Quotient Self-Assessment

This 19-question self-assessment will help you determine the innovation quotient for your organization. All 19 questions are derived from the material presented in this book. There is a quick reference "answer guide" at the end of this appendix that maps each question to the most relevant portions of the book where you can find more information.

Appendix B: Quick Notes

This appendix aggregates the Bottom Line (see Book Conventions) section from each chapter into one place for quick reference.

Book Conventions

Side Boxes, which are sprinkled throughout the book, are sections that are specifically separated from the main body of the chapter and provide additional relevant and interesting information to the topic being discussed in that chapter.

Callouts highlight a line or two (may be paraphrased) that are crucial to the topic being discussed. Think of call outs as "MTV sound bites."

The Bottom Line is the last section of each chapter that summarizes the three key points of that chapter. It also provides a quick and easy reference to the chapter for the future.

Audience

The book is intended for anyone who is responsible for innovation within their organization. That means it includes everyone from senior executives to task-oriented employees since "innovation is everyone's job" in our globally competitive economy. Furthermore, the content of this book applies to all whether you are in the private, public, or nonprofit sector. There are no prerequisites and the assumptions I make of you are simple – you want to innovate and are open to new ideas. In return I promise to give it to you straight – no jargon and no beating around the bush.

The simple fact is that we are all innovators at heart. All of us have had those moments in life where we've solved a problem – big or small – in a way that was unique, made us proud, and put a smile on our face, even if it did just entail using duct tape in a way that it wasn't ever intended! It is my hope that as you read the pages of this book, it will help you better express the innovator inside you and ultimately help you prosper in this new era – The Innovation Age.

Part I

A New Era

Most experts agree that we have entered into a new era where innovation is no longer a luxury or an option. Rather, continuous innovation is now the new norm. Regardless of your industry (private, public, or nonprofit) and what your role is, innovation applies to everyone in the Innovation Age. Part 1 walks you through the intricacies of this bold new era of continuous innovation. It not only explains why innovation is so crucial for survival in our globally competitive economy but provides insight into the true purpose of innovation – both in theory and in practice.

1

Introducing the Innovation Age

Just a decade ago, Blockbuster ruled the movie rental business. With over 25,000 employees at 8,000 stores and a distribution system of 6,000 DVD vending machines, it was valued at $8 billion in 2005. In September 2010, just one month short of the 25th anniversary of the opening of its first store, Blockbuster filed for bankruptcy. An upstart called Netflix had successfully managed to uproot Blockbuster from its throne in the movie rental business. It did so by fundamentally changing the delivery model for movie rentals from physical DVDs to streaming media. While Blockbuster was filing for bankruptcy in 2010, Netflix's market value had soared to a whopping $13 billion.

Today, less than two years later, Netflix is facing a dilemma of its own. Competitors such as Dish Network, Google, Amazon, and Hulu are trying to usurp Netflix by changing the rules of the game just as Netflix did to Blockbuster only a few years ago. While it is too early to say if they will succeed, Netflix is already feeling the effects. Since July 2011, Netflix has lost more than 500,000 subscribers and $9.5 billion in market value. Is this history repeating itself, albeit at a much quicker pace? Is this déjà vu?

Welcome to the Innovation Age.

As you will see in the next few pages, the stories about what Blockbuster went through and what Netflix is currently going through are not unique. Rather, these stories represent the cold, hard reality of the new rules for the "survival of the fittest" in the Innovation Age.

That was the beginning of the Information Age. Finally, your journey ends back in the present time where the dawn of the 21st century has brought yet another step change. You have just entered the Innovation Age and as you will quickly find out the rules of survival have changed considerably. The question is will these new rules favor you?

The Innovation Age is fundamentally unique from any of the previous ages that we have been through. For one, compared to the previous ages, there is less reliance on the left-brained processes of logic and knowledge, and more reliance on the right-brained processes of intuition and creative thinking. Daniel Pink provides many thought provoking example of this shift from the left- to the right-brain in his book, *A Whole New Mind* (Pink, 2005).

What is most unique about the Innovation Age is the change in the role of innovation itself.

Perhaps what is most unique about the Innovation Age is the change in the role of innovation itself. While in previous ages innovation was that "step change" that led mankind from era to the next, innovation is now an ongoing activity. As C. K. Prahalad and M. S. Krishnan write in their landmark book, *The New Age of Innovation* (Krishnan & Prahalad, 2008), the keys to creating value and growth in the 21st century depend on how well companies can reinvent their processes and culture to continuously seek innovative solutions. Even United States President Barack Obama, in his 2011 State of the Union address (The White House, 2011), challenged his country to win the future by "out-innovating" the rest of the world. Indeed, in an era where mass customization and mass personalization have been replaced with the need for mass innovation, prospering in the Innovation Age requires the ability to constantly innovate. "Out-innovating," as President Obama so eloquently put it, is the essence of what the Innovation Age is all about.

Continuous Innovation – The New Norm

The stories about companies such as Atari, Sony, Palm, Motorola, and Blockbuster illustrate an important and distinguishing fact about the Innovation Age – continuous innovation is the key to creating a sustainable competitive advantage. To continue to remain competitive in the Innovation Age, the product or service must continue to provide real value to the customer, be differentiated from competitors' offerings, and present a significant barrier to imitation. Charles Darwin described the essence of innovation in his "survival of the fittest" (Darwin, 1859) theory, in which he contended that it's not

> *To survive and maintain competitive advantage in the Innovation Age, companies must continuously innovate.*

always the strongest, or fastest, or biggest species that survive but the ones that are the most versatile and adapt to their changing environment. In other words, all species must continuously innovate to evolve. If they don't, they simply won't survive; it's as simple as that.

The message for organizations to prosper in the Innovation Age is equally simple, loud, and clear: To survive and maintain competitive advantage in the Innovation Age, companies must continuously innovate. Gillette is an example of a company that has consistently dominated its core market of personal care and grooming through continuous innovation, which is clearly reflected in its corporate mantra of "Innovation is Gillette."

Gillette is the pioneer of the business model of "giving away the handle and making money on the blades." This model has been copied by many industries since. For example, inkjet printer manufacturers have adopted this model to sell printers for next to nothing or even give them away for free with a computer with the expectation of making money on the lucrative, high-margin ink cartridges.

Gillette, in fact, has taken the concept of "out-innovation" to a new level by constantly cannibalizing its own products, such as its Sensor and Mach3 shaving product lines. Both these products lines have gone through many innovative changes over the years. According to professor Gurprit S. Kindra of the University of Ottawa's Telfer School of Management, the primary reason Gillette is successful is because "of its attitude of continually rejuvenating existing products with new features to stay ahead of its competitors." Gillette's ability to continuously out-innovate its competitors as well as itself is its key to prospering in the Innovation Age.

Innovation Applies to All

So far we have talked about the importance for companies to continuously innovate in the Innovation Age so that they not only create but maintain their competitive advantage over time. Intuitively, this makes sense for private sector companies seeking to maximize their bottom line profit. But does this apply to the public sector (federal, state, and local government) and nonprofit organizations such as the Red Cross and United Way? After all, if the purpose of innovation is to create and sustain competitive advantage then is it really applicable to them? The short answer to the question is a resounding "Yes."

> *Innovation applies to all — whether you are in the private sector, public sector, or a not-for-profit organization.*

Competitive advantage is a relative term. In the private sector, it typically translates to anything that helps a service or product provider make higher profits. In the public sector and for nonprofit organizations, however, competitive advantage is about providing best value (efficient and cost-effective) services to constituents and those in need. Innovation in the public sector might mean that an agency provides a wider range of services to its constituents, or the same service faster, better, or cheaper. Similarly, for nonprofit organizations, innovation is key to finding new ways of providing more to those who need aid with the same amount of resources.

As you will see in the following pages, creative problem solving and innovation are as crucial in the public sector and nonprofit organizations as they are to the private sector. Innovation and the resulting competitive edge in these areas are about providing best value (efficient and cost-effective) services to constituents and those in need respectively. It is about driving real performance improvements by not necessarily doing more of the same thing faster and cheaper but by finding new and novel ways to solve old problems. In the Innovation Age, innovation applies to all – whether you are in the private sector, public sector, or a not-for-profit organization.

Innovation in the Public Sector

Just over a decade ago, the U.S. Federal Government boasted back-to-back years of record budget surpluses. Those days are long gone and we are now in a period of public sector austerity where state governments are struggling to balance their budgets and the nation is embroiled in a raging debate over the debt ceiling, the growing federal deficit, and the size and scope of federal government. The U.S. is not alone in facing these challenges. In fact, the entire global economy is facing a financial crisis of historic proportions that involves banking systems, stock markets, and the flow of credit. Not surprisingly, there is a constant pressure on the public sector to reduce waste, eliminate bureaucracy and, in general, do more with less. Discussion about how to improve government-run services and how elected officials can save money and create jobs is rampant. Doing so will require the public sector to diligently employ innovative ways of partnering with and empowering its constituents to help agencies formulate effective policies and deliver efficient services (see the Side Box "Innovation's Sinking Fortunes in the United States" on page 18).

There are many examples of innovative public/private partnerships reaping significant benefits. For example, consider a longstanding challenge that the Federal Government had faced about unlocking the value of the vast amount of data that it has about its constituents. Rather than continuously trying to anticipate the needs of different constituent groups and playing "catch up," they decided to publish the data online to make it easy for anyone to remix and reuse the data, thus involving the American people in solving their own problems in creative ways.

To spur innovation, the Obama Administration has encouraged departments and agencies to experiment with new technologies such as Cloud Computing that have the potential to increase efficiency and reduce expenditures (Miller, 2011).

Many in the public sector are leveraging the power and reach of social media as they search for innovative ways to communicate with their constituents. A prime example is the City of San Francisco, which over the last two years has aggressively embraced social media sites such as Twitter, Facebook, and YouTube for marketing of government programs and initiatives, citizen engagement, and two-way communications (Hampton, 2011).

Innovations don't have to be technology centered. An example of a useful but low-tech innovation can be found in the City of Louisville that has created one-stop centers where residents can access healthcare, employment, and educational organizations in one trip (Jana, 2009). Think of it as a "mall" for solving urgent medical and job-related problems.

Innovation in Nonprofit Organizations

Nonprofit organizations have a difficult job. Not only must they ensure that they are providing effective and efficient services to those in need but they must fiercely compete for each charitable dollar. After all, we all have a choice of where we donate our time, possessions (food, clothes, etc.), and money. Contenders include organizations such as the Red Cross and United Way, local charities, and religious institutions. Each of these must continuously find innovative ways of providing aid to those in need while showing that they are maximizing the "help" potential of each dollar received (i.e., most of it goes to the needy as opposed to administrative costs). They must also find innovative ways of reaching potential donors, especially during crisis situations. Just as in the public sector, many are turning their attention to social media. For example, in the chaotic hours following the devastating earthquake that hit Japan in March 2011, many aid organizations turned to Twitter and Facebook asking their followers to send texts that would instantly pledge a small donation—$10 in most cases—to help the relief effort. Organizations such as the American Red Cross, Global Giving and Save the

Children provided followers with information about the loss of lives and property, along with their pleas for donations (Wallop, 2011). Meanwhile, Twitter and Google's online Person Finder tool gave aid organizations a method to gather information about the disaster and correct any misinformation on the Web.

Ushahidi is another example of an innovation that has helped save many lives in disaster struck areas such as Haiti and Chile. It all started in 2008, while Kenyan blogger Ory Okolloh was covering the post-election violence in Kenya and she blogged, "Any techies out there willing to do a mash up of where the violence and destruction is occurring using Google Maps?" Within days, two such techies wrote software code for an open-source, Web-based platform that would come to be known as Ushahidi, which means "testimony" in Swahili. Ushahidi provides volunteers information collected from a variety of sources that include text messages, blog posts, videos, phone calls, and pictures, all mapped in near real time. Over 10,000 Haitian-American volunteers across the United States translated every text message from Creole to English within 10 minutes. The result of this innovation has been nothing short of spectacular with countless precious lives saved.

Innovation can also help nonprofits proactively improve the quality of life for those less fortunate. For example, in poorer communities with cramped settlements of small metal roofed houses a common problem is that most, if not all, sunlight gets blocked out of their homes. Not only does this pose a challenge for performing the simplest of household chores such as cooking, but the dark, damp areas become fertile breeding grounds for mold and other disease causing agents. To help the thousands of poor families in Manila that suffer from this exact problem, students from the Massachusetts Institute of Technology created the solar bottle bulb – a simple, yet effective innovation that requires a one-liter soda bottle filled with a mixture of purified water and bleach. The bottle is inserted halfway through a hole drilled in the metal roof. The bleach "poisons" the water to keep molds from developing so the mixture lasts up to five years. The clear, purified water disperses the light through refraction. This makeshift, innovative light bulb costs less than $3 to make and provides approximately 55 watts of light! By 2012 more than a million homes in the Philippines will have daylight thanks to this simple but powerful innovation (Solar Bottle Bulb).

Innovation's Sinking Fortunes in the United States

Why is the Ocean getting higher?

In July 2011, the Information Technology and Innovation Foundation issued its latest report (Atkinson & Andes, 2011) on the state of United States' innovation-based competitiveness compared with a group of 44 countries. The report rates the innovative abilities of the 44 countries Using 16 key indicators from six broad categories that include human capital, innovation capacity, entrepreneurship, IT infrastructure, economic policy, and economic performance. Factors that are evaluated include a range of things such as a country's scientists and engineers, corporate and government R&D spend, available venture capital, productivity and trade performance.

The news isn't so good for the United States. The latest report finds that America has made little or no progress since 1999. Furthermore, of the 44 countries, the United States ranks fourth behind Singapore, Finland and Sweden. This doesn't sound so bad until you consider the fact that just 10 years ago America was at the number one position!

Even more concerning, though, is the downward death spiral of America's progress in improving her innovation capacity and competitiveness over the last decade. In fact, America is near the bottom of the list of countries where innovation is seen as improving.

Innovation's Sinking Fortunes in the United States
Continued

At the top of the "improved" list are countries such as China, South Korea, Cyprus, Slovenia, and Estonia. This means that if current trends continue, we could have a significantly different top 10 innovating countries list in the near future with the United States clearly out of the top 10.

According to the report, America's challenge is not necessarily a lack of willingness to change. Rather, the report summarizes it as the false belief that since the United States has been number one for so long it will continue to be number one regardless of whether it acts decisively.

This false sense of security is, what the report contends, why America believes that there is no real need to develop and implement a national innovation-based competitiveness strategy, but simply focus on maintaining the status quo market forces such as supporting free trade, restricting monopolies, simplifying the tax code, and deregulation. In short, to paraphrase the report, America is "seduced by its own success."

The current economic downturn coupled with a soaring national debt isn't helping either. The resulting U.S. cost cutting culture has effectively stalled all projects that don't show an immediate ROI or reduction in spending.

Granted, today's tough times require effective and efficient management of the present, but the in the Innovation Age the future will belong to those countries that can create it through innovation, global competitiveness, and leadership.

So, What Is Innovation Anyway?

Webster defines innovation as "the introduction of something new – a new idea, method, or device." Although the word innovation is about novelty, neither the concept nor the word itself is novel. Management guru Peter Drucker talked about innovation more than 25 years ago in *Innovation and Entrepreneurship* (Drucker, 1993) as "the specific instrument of entrepreneurship and the act that endows resources with a new capacity to create wealth."

But the origin of the word innovation goes much further. In fact, various sources including Webster, Dictionary.com, and Wikipedia put the origin of the word in the 1540s. According to Wikipedia, the word innovation is derived from the Latin word *innovationem*, which is the noun form of the verb *innovare*. The word *innovare*, as explained in the Etymology Dictionary, stems from the Latin word *innovatus*, which literally translates as "to renew or change into new." The literal definition of innovation is therefore "the process that renews something that exists" and not, as is commonly assumed (such as in the Webster definition above), the introduction of something new.

So, if innovation is not just about "newness," then what is its true meaning? In *Managing Creativity and Innovation*, Richard Luecke and Ralph Katz (Leucke & Katz, 2003) define innovation as "the successful introduction of a new thing or method and the embodiment, combination, or synthesis of knowledge in original, relevant, valued new products, processes, or services." Therefore, as summarized in Equation 1, Innovation is a function of both Invention ("new") and Commercialization, where the combination of the practicality of the invention and the ability to commercialize it is a measure of its value.

Equation 1: Innovation = Function (Invention, Commercialization)

Figure 2: Value is what bridges the gap between an invention and innovation.

As shown in Figure 2, this concept of "value" is what distinguishes a true innovation from a mere invention and is ultimately what provides the innovator with a sustained competitive advantage. In the private sector, "value" might translate to a higher top line (increased revenues, increased shareholder value, etc.) while as we saw in the previous section, in the public and nonprofit sectors "value" typically means more effectively achieving the mission objectives (serving constituents and those in need of aid).

The Customer Centric Paradox

By now you've probably realized two key facts about innovation: one, its primary role is to create sustainable competitive advantage and two, it must provide "value" to be distinguished from a mere invention. Obviously, that implies that innovation must keep the customer at the center of all activities. After all, how many times have we heard that to be successful, innovation must be driven by customers, or in other words it must be "customer centric"? But what exactly does "customer centric" mean?

The real meaning of the term "customer centric" is not what is commonly assumed and in fact, it is this [false] assumption that often dooms innovation from the very get go. This is what I refer to as the "customer centric" paradox. Real customer focused innovation does not mean blindly following the customer but rather intimately understanding the "job" they are trying to accomplish. This concept is best illustrated in the form of a story.

Figure 3: The Customer Centric Paradox.

Apple introduced the iPad in January 2010. Three months later in April within just 28 days of going on sale, Apple sold one million units. It is a phenomenal success story indeed attributed to the unique vision that Steve Jobs had.

Or was it a unique vision?

Actually, years before Steve Jobs had even thought of the iPad, Bill Gates had already foreseen the power of such a device. Back in November 2001, Gates boldly declared that just as the PC had taken computing from the back office to everyone's office, so would the tablet change the world by making PC like capability available to anyone, anywhere. He further predicted that within five years the tablet would be the most popular form of PC sold within America (Gates, 2001).

A few months later the first Tablet PC was born. Essentially, it was a pen-based, fully functional x86 PC with handwriting and voice recognition functionality. In fact, the Tablet PC used the same hardware as a normal laptop but added support for pen input. The launch was lukewarm and nowhere close to the success that the iPad had eight years later.

What happened?

There are many reasons the Tablet PC launch was not as successful as it could or should have been. There are many stories about Microsoft's failure to pioneer a truly innovative mobile version of Windows because of

Real customer focused innovation does not mean blindly following the customer.

the very strong and profitable fiefdoms within. For example, former Vice President Dick Brass explained in an opinion piece in the New York Times how the vice president in charge of Microsoft Office at the time refused to modify Office applications to work properly on the Tablet PC (Brass, 2010).

Perhaps, the most critical of failures is Microsoft's misinterpretation of the true meaning of "customer centric." When most people hear the term customer centric they immediately think of focus groups. At Apple, focus groups are taboo. As Steve Jobs once said, "It's not about pop culture and it's not about fooling people, and it's not about convincing people that they want something that they don't" (Jobs, 2008). Apple does not believe in asking

The customer centric paradox boils down to the simple fact that most customers simply do not know what they really want in a new product.

their customers what the next big thing is because figuring that out is Apple's job.

The customer centric paradox boils down to the simple fact that most customers simply do not know what they really want in a new product. If Apple had used focus groups the iPad might have looked more like the Tablet

PC, which was essentially a smaller, less capable laptop. It might have been more expensive, perhaps heavier, probably not as sleek and elegant, definitely much more capable (with Adobe Flash☺), and might have even included a keyboard. Instead, Apple introduced a product that took the market by pleasant surprise.

The reason focus groups rarely lead to truly innovative products, but only lead to incremental improvements to existing products is because customers don't innovate; they iterate. Most focus groups suffer from "group think" in which the final consensus ends up being a compromise between the most

> *Innovation is not about a faster horse.*

vocal customers and the company's grand vision. As innovation expert Robert Verganti reminds us, trying to make everyone happy only results in disappointment for all. This is exactly why a compromise, as most management experts agree, is essentially a "lose-lose" situation in which none of the parties involved get what they are looking for.

The customer centric paradox is best captured in a classic quote from Henry Ford in which he says, "If I asked my customer what they wanted I would have built a faster horse." But innovation is not about a faster horse; it's about meeting unmet customer needs with solutions that customers might not have thought about. Imagine if you were a company that manufactured VCRs back in the 1980s and mid-1990s and you asked your customer what they wanted. What do you think they would have said? After all, what was the biggest frustration with VCRs? I believe most of us dreaded rewinding the tapes. That might have prompted you to manufacture a VCR that rewound tapes faster. Now, I bet that if you had spent all your energy on creating a faster rewinding VCR, you would have really dreaded the DVD player!

Let's play another game of "imagine this." Let's say you are a soft drink company and a key rival starts creating ad campaigns around a test in which consumers are blindfolded and given both your and their soft drinks to determine which one they prefer blindfolded. Time and time again these blindfolded consumers choose your rival over you. What would you do? Would you change your soft drink to be more like your rival's? After all, that's what your customers want, right?

As it turns out, pursuing that course of action might be a major disaster as evidenced by Coca-Cola's introduction and subsequent failure of its New Coke. Surprisingly, Coca-Cola is responsible for one of the biggest blunders in marketing - New Coke (Snopes.com). New Coke was introduced because in blind taste tests of 200,000 respondents, most people preferred Pepsi to Coke. The revelation was startling to Coca Cola and they decided that it was time to change their formula to make it sweeter like Pepsi. After months of tweaking the formula, doing blind taste tests, research and changing their packaging, New Coke was launched. The resulting consumer backlash was devastating.

How did Coca-Cola misjudge the market to this extent after spending $4 million and more than two years to test a reformulation of Coke? There have been many studies conducted to conclusively answer that very question. Most studies concluded that consumers choose Coca-Cola not just because of its taste but due to a deeper psychological association based on tradition and loyalty. In other words, consumers' true feelings run even

> *True innovation happens when a company really understands the "job" a customer is trying to accomplish.*

deeper than they themselves realize leading us once again to the "customer centric" paradox.

As illustrated by the story about Apple and its success with the iPad, the key to a successful customer centric approach is realizing that customers simply want to do a "job." As Peter Drucker has famously said, "The customer rarely buys what the business thinks it sells him." True innovation only happens when a company really understands the "job" a customer is trying to accomplish using the company's product or service and then focuses all its efforts in helping the customer perform their "job" more efficiently be it simpler, faster, or cheaper. But if customers may not even know what they want, is it still necessary to solicit their input? The answer is an absolute yes. Understanding the "job" a customer is trying to accomplish requires direct input from the customer. Principle 4 (Innovation Seeks to Be Free) in Part 2 talks about how innovation seeks to be free by soliciting ideas from everyone and everywhere, including customers and even competitors. The customer centric paradox does not discourage soliciting input from customers; it discourages blindly following customers to their perceived solution. Real innovation is about filling a gap that customers don't even know they have. Apple has changed the world because it started innovation with the goal of making people more creative and more productive in their "jobs."

Another example of customer centric innovation that did not rely on focus groups but rather on understanding what the customers really wanted (i.e., their "job") is the story of how the popular game Cranium was created.

During a vacation in the Hamptons, Richard Tait and his wife, Karen, who were unbeaten in Pictionary, were challenged to a game of Scrabble®. The Taits were beaten pretty badly, which ultimately caused Richard to wonder what it would be like if there were a game that would make all players feel like winners.

That game is what we know now as Cranium® – a game that has received the prestigious "Game of the Year" designation at New York's Toy Fair and was later sold to Hasbro for almost $80 million.

> *Failure to motivate "the majority" to change the status quo is a root cause of why many companies struggle with innovation.*

Cranium is the perfect example of a customer centric innovation. A focus group would never have resulted in the creation of a game such as Cranium. Cranium was born because Richard Tait understood the "job" of his customers when they played a game – they wanted to feel good about themselves. So, just as Apple is not in the computer business but in the business of making their customers more creative, Cranium too was not in the business of selling games but rather in the business of raising self-esteem.

Prospering in the Innovation Age

By now one fact should be abundantly clear — we are squarely inside a new era of innovation — the Innovation Age. Having said that, the question then becomes, "how does one survive and prosper in this new era?" Before we answer that question, let's take a slight detour to understand the challenges innovation often faces.

In *The Economy of Cities*, Jane Jacobs says that if a flying saucer came to Earth she'd want to know how they avoided stagnation (Jacobs, 1970). The main battle in any society, according to Jacobs, is not between rich and poor or owners and labor, but between those who benefit from the status quo and those who benefit from new ways of doing things. Over time the status quo becomes even more powerful as more and more people become part of the majority. This is typically the beginning of the death of innovation.

> *Status quo is the enemy of innovation.*

The moral here is that if you keep doing the same things, but more intensely, you will grow in conventional economic terms (e.g., GDP) but you aren't solving your problems. Doing more of the wrong thing (e.g., treating all diseases with pills) counts as growth but in the long run such growth makes things worse, not better, because the "bad" ways of doing things just become further entrenched.

The failure to motivate "the majority" to change the status quo is a root cause of why many companies struggle in the Innovation Age to even get their innovation initiatives off the ground. In other words, status quo is the enemy of innovation.

Changing the status quo requires a culture shift in which innovation and constant adaptation are seen as the new way of life, or the new status quo. I discuss this more in Part 3. A few organizations (or pockets therein) are able to overcome the initial cultural inertia but yet fail to produce any substantial innovations. The five principles of innovation discussed in Part 2, and based on my experience and research, are aimed directly at aiding organizations overcome that dilemma. In addition, the principles address common myths of innovation such as:

- ✘ The hardest part about innovation is coming up with a great idea.

- ✘ Only the best ideas can lead to successful innovations.

- ✘ Successful innovations are the result of gifted people having groundbreaking epiphanies.

- ✘ Successful innovators rarely fail. If an implementation of an idea fails it cannot be innovative.

- ✘ Innovation is the responsibility of the "R&D" department

- ✘ Innovation cannot happen in a constrained environment

- ✘ A product of a service is innovative only if it creates a completely new market

Principles 1 and 2, for example, discuss how successful innovation is more about the implementation of an idea than the idea itself and that failures are just milestones along a long journey to success. As an example, consider how many of us enjoy relaxing in our hot tubs after a long day of hard work. But did you know that we were almost denied of this luxury? In the 1950s the Jacuzzi brothers invented a whirlpool bath to treat people with arthritis. Although it was a great idea and the product worked, it was a sales flop. The reason is that few people in the target market – sufferers from arthritis – could afford the expensive bath. Had the Jacuzzi brothers given up, we might not be enjoying our hot tubs today. Fortunately for us, they tried re-launching the same product for a different market – as a luxury item for the wealthy. The rest, as they say, is history.

So, without further ado, let's move on to the next section where we will start looking at each of the five principles in much more detail.

The Bottom Line

✓ We have already entered the Innovation Age in which the new norm is continuous innovation. Innovation is not an option nor a luxury but the new way of life.

✓ Innovation is not about a faster horse; it is about really understanding what the customer's needs are. At the same time, beware of the customer centric paradox.

✓ Innovation applies to all – whether you are in the private sector, the public sector, or a not-for-profit organization.

Part 2

Five Principles of Prosperity

Today, the question perplexing most organizations is not if we have entered a new age of continuous innovation but how to thrive and prosper in this new era. The innovation age is fundamentally different from previous ages in that innovation is not an option but an absolute necessity for survival in today's extremely competitive and global economy. This section introduces five principles based on research and years of experience that can help organizations prosper in this fundamentally unique era.

1   **Innovation is one percent ideation and 99 percent implementation.**

2   **Innovation is a journey not a destination.**

3   **Innovation is "where no man has gone before."**

4   **Innovation seeks to be free.**

5   **Innovation has many forms.**

2

Innovation Is One Percent Ideation and 99 Percent Implementation

When most people think about innovation, they immediately associate successful innovation with great ideas. But such thinking actually inhibits innovation. Yes, ideas are an essential ingredient, but they are only a small part of the recipe for innovation.

Over a hundred years ago, Thomas Alva Edison told us that genius is only one percent inspiration and 99 percent perspiration. A century later, Vijay Govindarajan and Chris Trimble reiterated this statement in *The Other Side of Innovation* (Govindarajan & Trimble, 2010), in which they discuss how turning ideas into actual breakthrough products, services and process improvements requires a trust-based partnership with the organization's performance engine.

Studies have shown that most companies fail, despite their creativity and technology expertise, because they do not convert ideas into reality. Having a great idea is akin to winning the first set in a five-set Grand Slam tennis match. Winning the first set can be exhilarating, especially against a top-ranked player such as Rafael Nadal or Roger Federer, but remember, you're only 33% done at best. To win the match, you have to sustain the high level of play for up to five sets.

> *An idea is an abstraction. To become useful it has to be implemented in some form – a product, a prototype, or a demonstration.*

Similarly, a successful innovation is not just a brilliant idea. Rather, as noted in Equation 1, executing a successful innovation requires both an invention and successful commercialization, which can only happen through dedicated implementation.

So, having a great idea is definitely an achievement, but implementing any idea to success is an even greater achievement. An idea is an abstraction. As Scott Berkun writes in *The Myths of Innovation* (Berkun, 2007), you can't get cash from simply the idea of an ATM. To become useful an idea has to be implemented in some form, such as a demonstration, prototype, or product. Even Google co-founder, Sergey Brin, insists that "Silicon Valley doesn't have better ideas and isn't smarter than the rest of the world, but it has the edge in filtering ideas and executing them" (Vaitheeswaran & Carson, 2007).

As we saw with Betamax and VHS, it's not always the best ideas that win. For example, Microsoft Windows is one the world's most dominant operating systems. It has evolved into a mature, robust, and capable operating system; but did it start out that way? It was neither the technically superior nor the most usable operating system during its early years. UNIX was technically superior and Apple's MAC OS was much more user-friendly; yet Microsoft Windows is the dominant operating system today. The key to its success is the company's sustained implementation efforts. In fact, had it not been for Bill Gates' tenacity, Windows (and for that matter, Microsoft), might not have even existed today. As author Harold Evans documents in his book, *They Made America*, a key reason why IBM approached Bill Gates was that Digital Research Inc. (DRI) founder Gary Kildall blew off IBM when they approached him to discuss licensing DRI's industry-leading operating system, CP/M (Evans, Buckland, & Lefer, 2004). This anecdote has been told so often that techies need only be reminded of "the day Gary Kildall went flying" to recall the rest.

Similarly, did you know that the original idea for Apple's MAC OS actually came from Xerox's PARC laboratories? The story is yet another example of how a company, in this case Xerox, clutched defeat from the jaws of victory. According to the story, Apple's Steve Jobs visited PARC labs to see their work on the graphical user interface (GUI) and saw the company's computer screens filled with icons, pull-down menus, multiple overlapping windows, and much more, all controlled by a click-and-point device, the mouse. The next time Jobs visited, he took his whole team. Xerox did not see the potential of its idea but Steve Jobs and Apple did. Apple followed through, the MAC OS was launched, and the rest, as they say, is history.

Ultimately, it doesn't really matter which idea was the best. All that matters in the end is which idea was implemented to success. Most computers today use a QWERTY keyboard (Figure 5), so-called because of the row of letters QWERTY. This keyboard was developed for early typewriters. But is it the keyboard most suited to modern computers?

If you were designing a keyboard, an important design principle is to make sure that most common words can typed with alternating hands to maximize efficiency of typing. That means while one hand is typing one letter, the other hand can position itself over the next letter and so on. In a QWERTY keyboard, however, not only is the left hand used more often, but more words can be typed only with the left hand than with the right hand.

Figure 5: The design of the QWERTY keyboard favors left-handed users.

The QWERTY keyboard clearly favors the left-handed user, yet less than 15% of the world's population is left-handed. So the QWERTY keyboard puts 85% of the population at a disadvantage! Despite that fact, the QWERTY keyboard has won the popularity contest over many other keyboard models that were superior in design and typing efficiency. When computers came into widespread use, the QWERTY keyboard continued to be used.

The essence of Principle 1 is best captured in a recent quote from Sir Howard Stringer, Chairman, President, and Chief Executive Officer of Sony. Talking about how Sony fell behind in the portable music device market, Stringer states that before Apple introduced the iPod in 2001, followed by the iTunes Music Store in 2003, Sony was already working with other companies on devices that download music. He summarizes the effort as, "Steve Jobs figured it out, we figured it out, we didn't execute." (Gruley & Edwards, 2011) Sony suffered from the same challenge that Xerox and DRI faced in the earlier examples. As was the case earlier, Sony stopped at the one percent ideation phase. Their fatal error was not following up with the 99 percent implementation, which as we know is crucial for successful innovation.

The Bottom Line

✓ The hardest part of innovation is not coming up with good ideas.

✓ No matter how good an idea is, it is just an abstraction. To be useful an idea must be implemented.

✓ Mediocre ideas can lead to successful innovation. The best ideas don't always win.

3

Innovation Is a Journey, Not a Destination

In Chapter 1, we saw that an innovation is much more than an invention. An idea can lead to an invention but transitioning that invention to an innovation requires evaluating and refining many different concepts through an iterative process of trials and errors.

Most of us have probably heard of WD-40. WD stands for water displacement. But what does 40 stand for? It represents the 40 attempts it took the Rocket Chemical Company to perfect this formula; that is, 39 earlier attempts failed.

How many of us have been on vacation to a place that is thousands of miles away? Yet, just over a century ago, few people would have contemplated traveling a thousand miles just for a few days. It was simply not possible. Modern day air travel has changed our lives forever. In 2005, in the United States alone, the general aviation sector contributed over $150 billion to national output, and directly or indirectly employed more than 1,265,000 people whose collective earnings exceeded $53 billion (MergeGlobal, 2006). According to the travel facts and statistics listed on the public website for the U.S. Travel Association, about 48 percent of U.S. adults traveled by air for leisure and business trips between August 2008 and July 2009.

The origins of modern day air travel can be traced back to December 17, 1903, when Orville Wright piloted the first powered airplane 20 feet above a wind-swept North Carolina beach. (Figure 6 shows an artistic rendition of the event.) The flight lasted 12 seconds and covered 120 feet. Three more flights were made that day with Orville's brother Wilbur piloting the record flight lasting 59 seconds over a distance of 852 feet.

What most people forget is that the Wright brothers tried over two hundred wing designs before they were successful. In fact, for years prior to their success in Kitty Hawk, the brothers experimented with kites, conducted hundreds of manned glider flights, and meticulously tested each of their designs in wind tunnels.

Figure 6: Orville Wright's first flight was preceded by intense study and hundreds of experiments.

Most of you probably are not surprised that something as complex as designing a functional airplane would require hundreds of iterations. But as my next example will illustrate the number of iterations is most certainly not a function of size. The Dyson vacuum cleaner is one of the best vacuum cleaners I have ever used. What I like most about the Dyson is that it actually makes vacuuming fun. No wonder James Dyson is a billionaire! After all, anyone who can make vacuuming fun for men deserves to be a billionaire. The story of how James Dyson created his vacuum cleaner is just as fascinating. According to the story, he became frustrated with the lousy suction of his vacuum cleaner while vacuuming his home. The bag and filter clogged too quickly, reducing the suction to the point where it didn't work. We all know the feeling but as we saw with other successful innovations in Principle 1 (Innovation Is One Percent Ideation and Ninety-Nine Percent Implementation), Dyson decided to do something about it. Over 15 years, he built 5,126 prototypes before he found one that worked.

There's no sugarcoating the fact that innovation is inherently risky; it is an iterative process requiring continuous refinement, building upon previous successes and failures. One reason is that innovation, as we saw in Equation 1, involves invention and commercialization, both of which are plagued with uncertainty and risk.

Thomas Edison famously said, "I have not failed. I have merely found ten thousand ways that won't work." This philosophy still rings true today as Tom Kelley of IDEO puts it, "Fail often to succeed sooner." Adam Richardson in his book, *Innovation X* (Richardson, 2010), quotes a study in which only one out of four product development efforts reap anything close to the desired benefits. A study by Jonathon Copulsky and Ken Hutt titled, "Gambling with the House's Money: The Randomness of Corporate Innovation," puts the numbers on success even lower (Copulsky & Hutt., 2006). Art Fry, the inventor of Post-it® notes describes innovation as a "numbers game in which you might have to go through 5,000 to 6,000 raw ideas to find one successful business."

> *Innovation is inherently risky; it is an iterative process requiring continuous refinement, building upon previous successes and failures.*

If innovation is so unpredictable then why is it perceived as a destination, as opposed to a journey? And why is this perception so pervasive? Perhaps because of the mismatch between what typically sustains an organization and what the organization needs to do to innovate. In fact, authors Govindarajan and Trimble contend that organizations are not designed for innovation, they are designed for efficiencies (Govindarajan & Trimble, 2010), which means that the inherently wasteful efforts to innovate conflict directly with the efficiencies-oriented mindset of organizations.

The key to successful experimentation and innovation is for teams to always seek the truth and not fall victim to the many organizational pressures to reach conclusions that are comfortable and convenient rather than analytical and dispassionate. For successful innovation to happen, corporate leadership and experimentation teams must understand and successfully resist these pressures.

A perfect example is of this understanding is Google's vision of "innovation, not instant perfection" (Salter, 2008), which allows the company to explore an idea by launching it early on Google Labs, iteratively learning what the market wants, and gradually taking the idea from good to great. Google also has an Innovation Time Out (ITO) policy that encourages employees to spend 80% of their time on

> *There is a fundamental mismatch between what typically sustains an organization and what the organization needs to do to innovate.*

core projects and roughly 20% (one day per week) on innovation activities that reflect their personal interests and passions.

Google's vision has resulted in many successful product launches. For example, Orkut, a popular social networking site in Brazil and India, was created by Orkut Büyükökten, a Turkish software engineer during his 20% ITO time. Another example is Google News, an automated news aggregator that is the result of work by the principal research scientist, Krishna Bharat in 2001. Krishna is attributed with creating StoryRank, related to Google's PageRank formula, in his 20% time. Other examples include the popular email program Gmail, and AdSense, an ad-serving application that has earned Google US$2.34 billion ($9.36 billion annualized), or 28% of its total revenue, in the first quarter of 2011 (Google Investor Relations, 2011).

Google is a good example of a company that recognizes that innovation is a journey and that the road to successful innovation may have potholes along the way. Take a look at its bumpy journey as it continues to try to establish a foothold in the realm of social media and networking. Orkut, the social networking site launched in 2004, has been sidelined by Facebook in most countries. Gmail, which was also launched in 2004 and whose invitations once sold for thousands on eBay, still lags significantly behind Hotmail and Yahoo Mail in total number of users. In 2007, Google bought Jaiku, a micro blogging service that was subsequently abandoned in 2008.

Meanwhile, Twitter, another micro blogging service, has prospered into a multibillion dollar business. Google Health is struggling and is slated to be discontinued in 2012. Google Wave was launched in 2009 as email 2.0, an attempt to build on the 2.0 bandwagon, and was suspended in 2010.

In February 2010, Google came out with Google Buzz, a social networking and messaging tool that is integrated into Gmail. It too has received a lukewarm response and has antagonized many over privacy violation issues. In fact, Google recently settled U.S. Federal Trade Commission charges that its social network, Google Buzz, violated the company's own privacy policies and used deceptive tactics when it launched in 2010. The FTC's main complaint was that Google used information collected from Gmail users to generate and populate Google Buzz and then automatically enrolled users in some features of the network regardless of whether they opted out, and worst of all, an auto-follow option automatically added Gmail users' most-emailed contacts as publicly visible friends on the network. The $8.5 million settlement also required Google to implement a privacy program and undergo regular privacy audits for the next 20 years (Forden & Womack, 2011).

Despite these challenges, Google continues to move forward in its quest of being a significant player in the social networking market. Since 2009, Google Maps has successfully overtaken MapQuest and Google's Android software has a 38% market share, which is higher than Apple's market share. In a testament to Edison's "I have not failed" quote, in June 2011, Google launched its latest foray in social networking with Google+, a Facebook-like site. So far there has been no backlash from privacy activists and within just two months it has over 20 million users signed up. Even Facebook founder, Mark Zuckerberg, has a Google+ account (Phillips, 2011)! Will Google+ succeed? The answer is not really important, for regardless of outcome, history has shown that Google will continue to march along on its journey of innovation.

The Bottom Line

✓ The road to successful innovation is paved with failures.

✓ Successful innovations are not necessarily the result of gifted people having groundbreaking epiphanies.

✓ Organizations are typically designed for efficiencies not innovation.

4

Innovation Is "Where No Man Has Gone Before"

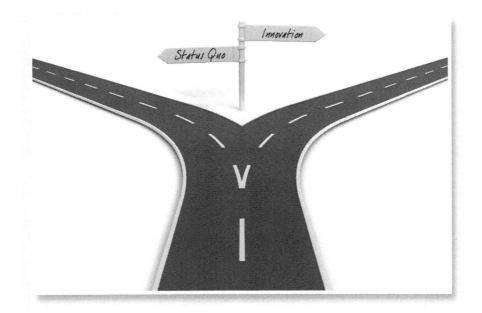

Most executives would give almost anything to fix their innovation process. It seems intuitive that if the company is not innovating enough there must be something wrong with its innovation process. However, as Richardson points out, "the problem is not innovation; the problem is the problem." (Richardson, 2010)

Richardson contends that companies' efforts to innovate are being thwarted by X-Problems, a new class of 21st century challenges that defy conventional planning.

Innovation is, as Star Trek fans would put it, "where no man has gone before." Going where no one has gone before requires out-of-the-box thinking. Innovation requires facing the tough and sometimes uncomfortable questions of "what if," "why not," and similar questions that challenge the status quo.

Every business faces many constraints that limit what it can and cannot do. Some constraints are imposed by the environment within which the business operates; some are imposed by laws and regulations that govern its products, services, and markets; yet others are imposed by the available technology at the time. Some constraints actually come from the consumers themselves in terms of what their buying patterns are, their tastes, and the price they are willing to pay. Finally, companies also face a slew of social requirements and expectations that may impose constraints on their operations..

> *Constraining factors can be the disruptive ingredient for game-changing innovations.*

But as Bhaskar Chakravorty explains in his article, Finding Competitive Advantage in Adversity, constraining factors can be the disruptive ingredient for game-changing innovations (Chakravorty, 2010). That's exactly what Cadbury India, now a subsidy of Kraft Foods, Inc., did in India while struggling to figure out the best way to sell chocolate in a market where temperatures are routinely above the 100 degree Fahrenheit mark. The problem, as one can imagine, is that chocolate and high temperatures are incompatible.

The constraint of high temperature provided the necessary platform for Cadbury India to launch Cadbury Bytes (Figure 7) and Chocki; each with melted chocolate in its core inside a protective casing of caramel that is not vulnerable to hot outdoor temperatures. These innovations have not only been highly successful in India, but have become a global hot seller for the company.

Figure 7: The design of Cadbury Bytes was developed in response to high temperatures (an environmental constraint).

Ravi Sandhu, professor at the Institute for Cyber Security at the University of Texas at San Antonio, has stated that, "compliance is a big burden on innovation." However, compliance is just another business environment constraint that is better viewed as a blessing in disguise.

Take for example cloud computing, which has grown from being a promising business concept (an idea) to one of the fastest growing segments (implementation) of the IT industry. Our current tough economic conditions and the constant pressure to accomplish more with less are prime catalysts for organizations to realize that tapping into the cloud can allow fast access to best-of-breed business applications and computing resources at negligible cost.

> *Sometimes innovation is spurred by imposing constraints where none currently exist.*

Private industry has taken the lead in developing the cloud computing market; however, many recent advances in cloud computing are attributed to government regulations around data center consolidation, security, and data privacy. So innovation can be used to overcome existing constraints.

On the other hand, sometimes innovation is spurred by imposing constraints where none currently exist. As an example consider the automobile market. People can spend a lot of money on their cars. For example, the Bugatti Veyron at $2,400,000 is by far the most expensive automobile on the market today. Next in line is the Pagani Zonda Cinque Roadster at $1,850,000, followed by the Lamborghini Reventón at $1,600,000. At the bottom of the top 10 most expensive production cars on the market is the Koenigsegg CCX at a mere $545,568 (The Super Cars, 2011).

But what about those people who can barely afford an average four-wheeler?

That is the constraint Indian industrialist Ratan Tata was thinking about when he challenged his engineers to design a "people's car" to retail for Rs. 100,000 (approximately $2,000-$2,500 USD), making it affordable for moderate income families. The result is the Tata Nano (Figure 8), a four door sedan that seats four to five people, is powered by a 33 horsepower, 624 cc engine and has a decent fuel economy of approximately 50 miles per gallon. The Nano was launched because of Tata's unwavering commitment to "question the unquestionable."

Figure 8: The Tata Nano is the result of an unwavering commitment to "question the unquestionable."

Another example of innovation spurred by imposing constraints involves one of the most basic human necessities – a roof over one's head. Affordable housing has long been both an aspiration and a gauge for economic equality within a society. While we have made significant progress in this area, the fact is that even in the most developed economies housing is typically affordable to only half of the population. According to David A. Smith, the founder of the Affordable Housing Institute (AHI), markets alone will never satisfactorily house a nation's poorest citizens. As proof he points to the "spontaneous community of self-built or informally built homes — the shanty towns, settlements, and ever-expanding slums that sprout like mushrooms on the outskirts of cities in the developing world." Back in August 2010, Vijay Govindrajan and Christian Sarkar issued a challenge to create a house for US $300 (Govindrajan,

> *History is full of examples of innovations that are the result of inquisitive (and dedicated) people asking questions that challenge the status quo.*

The $300 House: A Hands-On Lab for Reverse Innovation?, 2010). The challenge has taken on a life of its own with many corporate sponsors, a website (300house.com), and many innovative design options for a "cheap" yet functional house. The winner, sponsored by Ingersoll Rand, was announced in June 2011 based on the voting results of the members of the online community at jovoto.com. The basic house cost just $293.80 (Vision Statement: The $300 House, 2011).

As a final example of price constraints serving as a potent fuel for innovation, consider the world of tablets. The average price of an Apple iPad based on a scan of Amazon.com is at least US $400. According to the Nations Online Project there are 16 countries that have a per capita income of less than US $1000 a year (Countries of the Third World - Nations Online Project). That means that an iPad is worth about five months of income, which is not a likely trade-off when balanced against other needs such as food, clothing, shelter, and health care. That poses an interesting dilemma. If the children of developing countries are not exposed to modern technology from an early age, the barriers to overcoming the increasingly steep digital divide will keep getting higher. To make sure even the poorest of Indian children has a shot at crossing over the digital divide, India has launched what it says is the world's cheapest touch-screen tablet computer, priced at just $35. The "Aakash" (translates to sky) tablet was developed by a UK-based company, DataWind, and the Indian Institute of Technology in Rajasthan. It supports web browsing and video conferencing and has two USB ports with a three-hour battery life. The Indian government plans to distribute 10 million of the devices to students over the next few years.

Figure 9: The Apple II Computer was the first computer designed for the general public.

History is full of examples of innovations that are the result of inquisitive (and dedicated) people asking questions that challenge the status quo. Apple's Steve Jobs was famous for continuously challenging the way things were. Apple's slogan of thinking differently captures his philosophy perfectly. Apple II (Figure 9) is widely heralded as the computer that launched Apple into the mainstream. But Apple II's revolutionary features were no accident. Rather, they were the result of a series of status quo challenging questions by Steve Jobs and his team of designers.

From the very beginning, Steve Jobs had the vision that unlike other computers of the time, Apple II would be a complete, ready-to-use computer marketed towards consumers rather than computing hobbyists. It was this vision of where no one had gone before that led to a series of game changing innovations, which ultimately made Apple II a blockbuster success. For example, Steve Jobs wanted Apple II to run quietly. At the time, computers were expected to be heard because it was a well-accepted fact that all computers needed a fan to prevent overheating. Challenging the status quo meant redesigning the power supply itself so that it generated less heat. The result, Apple II, featured a power supply that did not require a fan, making it the quietest and smallest computer on the market at that time.

Jobs also questioned why computers at the time looked the way they did. Jobs realized that for the computer to be marketed to the general public, its design needed to be as familiar as a kitchen appliance, such as a Cuisinart food processor. Even the advertisement introducing Apple II was set in a kitchen with a man resting his hand on his Apple II and a woman standing at a sink and smiling at him. This concept was entirely novel and marketed the computer to the general public with the premise that computing is easy, fun and productive. It was truly where no one had gone before!

The Bottom Line

✓ Innovators never shy away from challenging the status quo with questions such as "what if," "why," and "why not."

✓ Constraints provide a fertile ground for innovation. Both existing constraints as well as imposed constraints can spur innovation.

✓ Innovation in one field is often the result of adopting "common" ideas from another field.

5

Innovation Seeks To Be Free

Why do some organizations seem better at innovating than others? Are these organizations just "born" better or can the culture and environment that encourages successful innovation be learned and acquired? For that matter, in what kind of environment does innovation thrive the most? The

known as one of the key U.S. government agencies behind the development of the internet, has been experimenting with "crowdsourced" solutions. In June 2011, it showcased a proof-of-concept, next-generation combat support vehicle (XC2V) that was completely designed and built as part of an open competition. And in October 2011, DARPA announced a new competition for the design, construction and manufacture of an advanced unmanned aerial vehicle (UAV) system.

Crowdsourcing and Open innovation are examples of innovation free from the constraints of "closed mind thinking."

Another example of unconstrained innovation is aptly called "open innovation," a term coined by Henry Chesbrough in his book, *Open Innovation* (Chesbrough, 2003). Open innovation encourages organizations to use external ideas in addition to internal ideas. We saw how Dell and Starbucks have successfully incorporated the principles of open innovation. Others too have experienced similar success (see the Side Box "What about Apple" on page 62).

For example, for years the United Kingdom's Department for Work and Pensions (DWP) struggled to figure out how to engage its more than 120,000 employees in innovative ways of accomplishing its mission of maximizing employment, reducing poverty, and promoting employment equality. Their solution entailed implementing an "open" and competitive market for ideas called "Idea Street" where employees could contribute, collaborate, and gain recognition for their participation in helping develop new ideas. Idea Street used a virtual currency that employees earned by commenting and trading (buying and selling) shares in ideas. The civil servant employee that eventually reached the top worked in a remote district office. As a result of his success in Idea Street, he received a letter from the Secretary of State for Work and Pensions to come and work in the central office (Burke & Mesaglio, 2010).

One more story might help illustrate the power of open innovation. A few years ago Procter & Gamble (P&G) had a problem with the packaging of one of its leading brands of laundry detergents in its European market. The detergent was sold in prepackaged pouches placed inside cardboard boxes. The problem was that about one out of every 1,000 pouches developed leaks that stained the cardboard boxes. Obviously customers would not buy the oily boxes. Sometimes the only boxes left on store shelves were the ones with stains. P&G was worried that this could affect their brand, so they assembled their top brains to figure out a solution. However, despite all their efforts, no one was able to come up with an answer. That's when Open Innovation came to the rescue. P&G approached NineSigma, an open innovation services provider who turned to its network of problem solvers.

The ultimate solution came from a small, not well-known company in the United Kingdom that produced agricultural concentrates such as herbicides and pesticides. It turned out this company was using the same water-soluble film to package some its products. Not surprisingly, they too had encountered the same problem but had found a way to overcome it during the packaging process. NineSigma played matchmaker and hooked the two companies up (see the Side Box "The Legal Side of Innovation on page 64).

This story illustrates just how powerful Open Innovation can be. The solution came from a place where P&G would never have thought to look. Used properly, open innovation can provide the swiftest and most effective answers. Companies spend millions of dollars in research and development to try to solve complex problems. But the people with the problems don't always know where to look for answers and end up spending money when the answer is already available somewhere.

> *P&G capitalized on Open Innovation because it had already gone through the organizational cultural shift of accepting ideas that did not originate within their organizational boundaries.*

P&G capitalized on Open Innovation because it had already gone through the organizational cultural shift of accepting ideas that did not originate within their organizational boundaries. Since its inception, P&G fueled its consumer products engine from research and development from within and, in fact, had one of the greatest research and development operations in corporate history.

What about Apple?

Back in Chapter 1, we saw how Apple consistently overcame the customer centric paradox by avoiding focus groups and instead relying on trained specialists to figure out what its customers really needed to do their "job". So, does Apple defy Principle 4?

While every principle might have an outlier exception, that does not seem to be the case here. Granted that Apple does not use "crowdsourcing" or "open innovation" per se, but many of its actions clearly show that it has embraced the philosophy of freedom of innovation. For example, Apple realizes that it cannot anticipate every need for every customer, which is why it opens the same software development kit it uses internally. This allows the "crowd" to build new applications for its devices. Is this not a form of "crowdsourcing" similar to what Vivek Kundra did with his Apps for Democracy contest?

Apple does not believe in focus groups but this in no way means that they do not want to hear from their customers. One reason why Apple launched its physical retail stores was so to engage their existing and potential customers directly and gain unfiltered insight into what their true needs are. These insights are gained by actively interacting with customers as they test drive various Apple products and work with customers to design solutions that fit their specific needs. Isn't this "open innovation" at its best?

Finally, in one of its first known public uses of the term "crowdsourcing," Apple recently claimed that it uses a "crowdsourced" database of nearby Wi-Fi hotspots and cell towers around a user's location. This allows Apple to quickly triangulate the user's position and lock on to GPS satellites and cell towers faster than any other method.

These examples clearly illustrate that Apple's success in innovation is not because it is "closed" in its innovation process, rather, because it has embraced the freedom of innovation in its truest sense.

But as the company grew to a $70 billion enterprise, the global innovation model that was at its core could not keep up with the rapid growth. By 2000, it was clear that P&G's invent-it-ourselves model was no longer capable of sustaining the high levels of top-line growth as it had become accustomed. The combined impact of new technologies, increased pressure on innovation budgets, flat research and development productivity, a stagnant innovation success rate (defined as the percentage of new products that met financial objectives), and newer, more agile competitors was devastating. P&G quickly lost more than half its market cap and its stock slid from $118 to $52 a share.

That's when CEO A. G. Lafley decided to broaden the horizon and look at external sources for innovation. The strategy was formalized as "connect and develop," leveraging technology and social networks to seek new ideas for future products. This strategy has helped P&G solve many of its most difficult challenges with innovative solutions. Today, more than 35 percent of P&G's new products have elements that originated outside the company, which is up from about 15 percent in 2000. P&G's research and development (R&D) productivity has increased nearly 60 percent, and its innovation success rate has more than doubled, while its cost of innovation has fallen. What makes these results even more astounding is the fact that their R&D investment as a percentage of sales is 3.4 percent, 1.4 percent lower than it was in 2000!

NineSigma is just one company that has capitalized on the recent willingness of organizations to look outside their companies for innovative ideas. There are many more. For example, the BIG Idea Group (BIG) boasts an open source network of 13,000 problem solvers and inventors ready to tackle almost any innovation challenge. BIG's network includes a variety of talent from industrial designers to marketing pros and experienced inventors.

Another such company is crowdSPRING that has "sprung up" to make crowdsourcing more accessible to the masses. crowdSPRING's network has more than 88,000 designers and writers from nearly 200 countries and a typical project gets about 110 entries, which pretty much guarantees a variety of innovative solutions from which project submitters can choose the most appropriate solution.

The Legal Side of Innovation

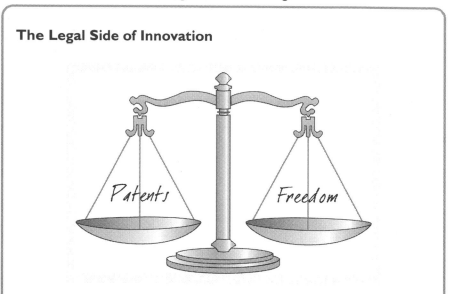

How do you protect your product or service from imitators who seek to take unfair advantage of your hard work?

Intellectual property (IP) is the area of law that deals with protecting the rights of those who create original works. IP laws cover everything from original plays, novels, and art, to inventions, innovations, and company identification marks. IP protection is critical to fostering innovation since it provides individuals and organizations with the assurance that their work will be protected and they will be able to reap the full benefits of their innovation.

The three primary mechanisms for protecting intellectual property are copyrights, patents and trademarks. Accordingly, it seems reasonable that the most innovative companies would also have the most copyrights, patents, and trademarks, right? Or could it be that the very concepts, laws, and regulations that were meant to encourage innovation are stifling it today?

Ask anyone to name some of the most innovative companies of our time and along with the familiar names such as P&G, Apple, 3M, etc., you are likely to hear names of rising stars such as Facebook, Twitter, Zynga, LinkedIn, and others. These newer additions to the list of most innovative companies have thrived on the emerging social

The Legal Side of Innovation
Continued

trends (such as open innovation), collaboration, and technology trends (such as cloud computing). While these emerging trends have provided a fertile ground for innovation to occur, one cannot help but wonder whether there is such a thing as a "free lunch."

In a recent article in *Businessweek*, there is one big difference between traditional innovators such as Microsoft, Oracle, and Apple, and the new generation, such as Facebook and Twitter – the number of patents these companies hold (Vance, 2011). The traditional innovators hold thousands of patents covering a vast number of areas from file and database management systems to fundamental technologies that make up our modern World Wide Web (WWW). Compare that to the patents held by companies in the newer cohort. According to filings with the U.S. Patent and Trademark Office Facebook has only 12 patents, while the totals for Twitter, Zynga, LinkedIn, and Groupon range from zero to two each (Vance, 2011). This potentially puts these newer companies at a legal disadvantage if, and, more likely, when the more established companies decide to take their battle from the innovation arena to the judicial arena.

In fact, this shift has already begun and even behemoths such as Google and Samsung are not immune. Just recently, Oracle has sued Google over the Android operating system with concerns that it violates Java patents (Krazit, 2010). Microsoft also has targeted several of Google's Android partners with patent infringement lawsuits (Gustin, 2011). Samsung and Apple have been locked in an acrimonious global battle over smartphone and tablet patents since April 2011 (Arthur, 2011). These lawsuits result in a feeding frenzy as companies – big and small – scramble to bolster their patent portfolios. Google has already spent billions on acquiring thousands of patents to defend against its mounting legal troubles (Wagner, 2011). Intellectual property law has become the proverbial "necessary evil" in this age of innovation.

Finally, InnoCentive is another example of a company that works with corporations of all sizes as well as the public and nonprofit sectors to help leverage open innovation and game style challenges to overcome their toughest dilemmas. To date, InnoCentive has posted over 1000 challenges to its community of over 250,000 problem solvers in 200 countries. These challenges come in all flavors.

One such challenge called "Vehicle Stopper" was issued by the Air Force Research Laboratory. The Vehicle Stopper challenge was looking for ways to stop a fleeing vehicle without causing permanent or severe injury to its occupants. The winning solution came from Dante Barbis, a retired 66-year-old mechanical engineer from Lima, Peru. Dante suggested an electric, remote-controlled robotic vehicle capable of accelerating to 130 mph within three seconds. This robotic vehicle would quickly catch up to the fleeing vehicle, deploy an airbag underneath it, lift the fleeing vehicle off the ground, and then slow it to a stop.

As in the case of P&G, with their dilemma around the leaky detergent pouches, Dante would have probably never even known about the problem nor would the solution he proposed have been found through traditional means.

The Bottom Line

✓ Innovation thrives in environments that encourage collaboration, participation, and open communication.

✓ Many successful innovations are the result of ideas that originated outside the organization.

✓ Organizations need to cultivate a culture in which innovation is everyone's responsibility not just of the chosen few in R&D labs.

6

Innovation Has Many Forms

What comes to mind when we think of innovation? Are you thinking about the impact that Ford's Model T had on the automobile industry in the early 1900s? Perhaps you are thinking about something more recent such as the effect of digital photography on the "point-and-shoot" camera market. Chances are that even if you are thinking of another example, it is more than likely an example of a type of innovation commonly known as a "disruptive innovation."

Disruptive innovation is a term coined by Clayton Christensen to describe a form of innovation in which a product or service initially takes root in simple applications at the bottom of a market and then relentlessly moves up market, eventually displacing established competitors (Christensen, The Innovator's Solution: Creating and Sustaining Successful Growth, 2003). It creates a new and unexpected market by applying a different set of values. Typical examples of disruptive

> *Disruptive innovation starts at the bottom on a market and then relentlessly moves upstream.*

innovation include the Ford Model T, digital photography, mini steel mills (such as Nucor), plastics, telephones, transistors, and the steam engine. Disruptive innovations have become so well known that there are Dilbert cartoon strips about it (Dilbert.com, 2004).

Unfortunately, Christensen's success in popularizing the term, in a way, has been a disservice to the field of innovation because it is the only perception of innovation most people have. However, this perception could not be further from the truth.

Innovation Avatars

The reality is that innovations come in many forms. An interesting analogy is found in Hinduism and the concept of avatar (Figure 10). Remember the 2009 blockbuster movie, Avatar? In the movie, Jake Sully is an ex-Marine who was wounded and paralyzed from the waist down. He comes to a moon called Pandora where his mind is linked with an "Avatar," a living, breathing body that can survive in the toxic Pandora atmosphere. The mind link allows Jake to control the "Avatar" as if it were his own body. The story is truly science fiction at its best.

Now, that I have most of you reminiscing on fond memories of the movie, I am going to ask you to "forget" that entire concept of "Avatar" for a moment. That's because avatars in Hinduism, which is in fact where the term originated, have no relation to the movie at all.

Figure 10: Vishnu with his 10 avatars (incarnations): Fish, Tortoise, Boar, Narsimha (Man-Lion), Dwarf, Rama with the Ax, King Rama, Krishna, Buddha, and Kalkin. Image source: Wikimedia Commons, Painting from Jaipur, India, 19th century; in the Victoria and Albe.

In Hinduism, an avatar is a descent of a deity from heaven to earth. The closest translation of the word in English is incarnation. The term is most often associated with Lord Vishnu, the preserver, though it has also come to be associated with other deities, such as Shiva and Ganesha. According to Hindu scriptures, Vishnu has taken many different avatars over the course of human civilization to protect the good and destroy evil. Each of Lord Vishnu's avatars is uniquely designed for a very specific purpose. Similarly, innovation too has many avatars, with none any better or worse than the other.

The lesson is that innovation has many different forms or avatars. It is not a one-size-fits-all proposition. So rather than worrying about the disruptiveness of an idea, an organization should focus on whether the idea can help create/sustain competitive advantage by adding value or meeting currently unmet customer needs (i.e., help to do the "job").

Even Christensen talks about a different "avatar" of innovation, called sustaining innovation that is not as radical as disruptive innovation and does not have an unexpected effect on existing markets. Sustaining innovations are incremental in nature and come in two forms: transformational and evolutionary.

> *Innovation has many avatars, with none any better or worse than the other.*

The automobile is a classic example of a transformational sustaining innovation. Early model automobiles were expensive luxury items that did not disrupt the market for horse-drawn vehicles. In fact, the market for transportation essentially remained intact until the debut of the lower priced (i.e., disruptive) Ford Model T in 1908, which made higher speed, motorized transportation available to the masses.

Conversely, an evolutionary innovation improves an existing product or service in an existing market in ways that customers are expecting. Going back to the automobile example, the introduction of a fuel injection engine to replace carburetors is an example of an evolutionary innovation.

Don't discount the value of such incremental innovation "avatars." Many modern luxuries that we take for granted are a result of minor tweaks to existing products and services. For example, most of us enjoy drinking our first cup of coffee in the car while driving to work. Well, the cup holder that allows us to do so safely without spilling hot coffee in our lap is an example of an incremental innovation avatar.

However, the classification of innovations as either disruptive or sustaining is just one example of how innovations can be categorized. There are many other classifications. Peter Fingar, for example, in *Extreme Competition*, describes six "avatars" of innovations: operational, organizational, supply-side, core-competency, sell-side, and product/service (Fingar, 2006).

And In *Dealing with Darwin*, Geoffrey Moore describes a taxonomy of fifteen innovation "avatars" based on a product's or service's maturity in its lifecycle (Moore, 2005). In this taxonomy, the popular disruptive innovation is most useful in growing markets,

> *Innovation is not a one size fits all proposition.*

but much less useful in mature and declining markets. Rather, the types of innovation most useful in mature markets would include line extension, value engineering, enhancement, integration, marketing experiential, and process or value migration. Along the same lines, the most useful innovation types in declining markets, according to Moore, would be organic renewal, acquisition renewal, or harvest and exit.

Innovation "avatars" are not just limited to new products and services or improving existing ones. Two such innovation "avatars" include Business Process Innovation and Business Model Innovation.

Business Process Innovation

Business Process Innovation occurs when organizations add value by fundamentally rethinking their internal business processes in order to create and sustain competitive advantage (see the Side Box "Social Media Cures Drug Maker's Ailing Supply Chain" on page 75).

For example, consider what managed healthcare provider Kaiser Permanente did to improve the quality of patient care. As nurses go on and off a shift, a crucial exchange of information and duties must take place to ensure safety, quality of care, and efficiency.

Looking to optimize the nursing shift change process within its hospital network, Kaiser Permanente partnered with design firm, IDEO. Rather than "paving the existing cow paths" with new technology solutions, the Kaiser Permanente-IDEO team conducted observations in four hospitals and watched shift changes around the clock in an attempt to understand the ways that information gets transmitted. The team supplemented its observations with a detailed understanding of other elements

Business Process Innovation involves adding value by fundamentally rethinking internal business processes.

that could affect the hand-off, such as staffing, bed management, patient transport, and different nursing roles.

A key finding was that every nurse had an individual way of prioritizing and communicating information; this meant that for any solution to be effective it would have to standardize the hand-off process around nursing schedules, information hand-offs, and patient interactions.

Ideation and brainstorming sessions followed in which nurses, doctors, and administrators participated. The resulting prototypes were tested for three weeks in a single unit during every shift change. Changes to the prototypes were made continuously, based on direct feedback from the nurses. Ultimately, the patients benefited from the more efficient hand-off procedures that allowed for better quality and safer care. These and similar business process innovations have helped Kaiser Permanente provide more efficient service to its members, reduce time spent in waiting rooms, and improve patient safety – all of which have earned praise from the Institute of Healthcare Improvement for Kaiser Permanente as the "best practice" in health care.

Social Media Cures Drug Maker's Ailing Supply Chain

Until just a few years ago, the Canadian operations of pharmaceutical company Ratiopharm, Europe's leading generic drug manufacturer, had major issues with the management of its supply chain.

Ratiopharm Canada found it increasingly difficult to react to changes in demand for its generic drugs. The problem was so severe that at times, the company was unaware for up to four months about manufacturing snafus or quality control issues that would affect downstream delivery of drugs to the market.

Careful analysis revealed that breakdowns in internal communication and information sharing prevented proactive decision making. That's when the company decided to use Web 2.0 and social collaboration tools to help employees share information more efficiently.

Social Media Cures Drug Maker's Ailing Supply Chain
Continued

Starting out with Microsoft's SharePoint, they incorporated collaboration tools from Strategy-Nets and enterprise social networking firm, Moxie Software. The results were so good that Ratiopharm's parent company Teva Pharmaceutical Industries also decided to adopt Ratiopharm's social media platform to fix its supply chain and service level problems.

Both companies have experienced dramatic improvements. Ratiopharm's service levels have gone up from around 82% to 95%. Meanwhile, the time to fill orders has decreased by over 60% from a whopping 80 days to 25-30 days (Gaudin, 2011). Teva has seen similar results with its service levels having improved substantially from w below 90% to close to 98%.

This story illustrates how a pharmaceutical company innovatively employed the power of social media to fix problems in its internal processes while most companies are still struggling to make the business case (mostly based on ROI) for even using social media for the simplest of things.

Business Model Innovation

In Part 1, we discussed how Sony is no longer the leader in the portable music market segment – a market space it created decades before but now struggles to maintain its relevance. This coveted top spot has now been claimed by Apple with its iPod series of MP3 players. But while the iPod series of MP3 players are quite innovative, they are not the main reason why Apple has taken leadership in this market. Almost all MP3 players use similar audio circuitry and there are several smaller, more compact, and sleeker looking MP3 players available on the market.

The real credit for Apple's success in this market actually goes to a different type of innovation known as business model innovation. Business model innovation refers to creating fundamental changes to an existing business model or coming up with a completely new one to meet customer's unmet needs. The iTunes Music Store platform that created an ecosystem where people could find and legally download high quality music files easily and reliably, share music with friends,

> *Business model innovation can be an effective way of creating and sustaining competitive advantage even in highly competitive, low tech market.*

and transfer them to multiple devices. The platform has grown over the years to include music videos, television shows, movies, and games. In fact, iTunes has become Apple's proverbial "foot in the door" into the extremely lucrative home entertainment market.

Business model innovation can be an effective way of creating and sustaining competitive advantage even in highly competitive, low tech market. In Chapter 1 we talked about a company, Gillette, which has done this very well over many decades. Gillette is famous for its "razor and blades" business model innovation, which boiled down to "giving away the handle and making money on the blades." The innovation was born when King Camp Gillette, the founder, was having trouble selling his marvelous new product, "disposable razor blades," in the early 1900s. Gillette decided to give away (for free) the razor handle that fitted the blades. His customers loved getting the free product, and since they "saved" so much on the handle, that they didn't mind spending on the disposable blades that went with it. After several blade purchases per customer, Gillette would make back what he lost on the handle - and then some. This loss-leader marketing strategy has been used by many organizations since then, most recently, by printer manufacturers who essentially give away their inkjet printers and make money on the expensive ink cartridges.

Another example of a business model innovation can be found with what Southwest Airlines does in the airline industry by offering a no frills flight alternative to customers. The real innovation is actually in how Southwest has managed to offer no frills flights with an employee-first culture that offers profit sharing and empowerment programs. This culture is what motivates the ground staff and flight crew to put passengers first, telling them jokes in the cabin and entertaining them with friendly behavior. Southwest's enviable success in an otherwise struggling airline industry has not gone unnoticed. Other airlines such as JetBlue, Ryanair, and easyJet have tried to imitate Southwest's business model to varying degrees of success. A few other examples of successful business model innovations include eBay's online auctions, Amazon's 1-Click ordering, IKEA's "do-it-yourself" furniture, University of Phoenix's degree programs for working adults, and NetJets' fractional ownership service to meet executives' occasional needs for private jet travel.

The Bottom Line

✓ Innovation is not a one-size-fits-all proposition.

✓ Innovation is not just limited to end user products and services,; innovation can also take the form of business model changes and internal or customer facing process improvements

✓ Regardless of the type of innovation, the ultimate focus must be on providing value and meeting currently unmet needs of your customers.

Part 3

Making Innovation Work
in Your Organization

Successful innovation takes more than a desire. While the concept of innovation itself is a noble cause, to be of real value (and contribute to the bottom line) the idea of innovation must be followed up with implementation. This is the challenge that keeps many senior leaders up at night. How does one implement the idea of innovation in their organization? In this section, I will discuss three techniques that have not only been shown to work in the most innovative companies of our time, but that I personally have used in my professional career to spur innovation with the companies that I have led.

1   **Instilling a culture of innovation**

2   **Leveraging the Medici Effect**

3   **Knowing what to measure**

7

Instilling a Culture of Innovation

Workplace culture is an important part of any organization because it affects everyone who is a part of or interacts with the organization, from employees to customers. It affects how things are done and, more importantly, why they are done in a particular way.

Every workplace has a culture, some of it deliberate and some cultivated. A positive workplace culture can allow an organization to thrive, while a dysfunctional culture can lead to an organization's downfall by pitting its employees against the establishment. As we saw in Part 2, innovation thrives in an open environment that views innovation as a journey and encourages taking measured risks. Workplace culture is the ultimate deciding factor on whether such an environment is even possible in an organization.

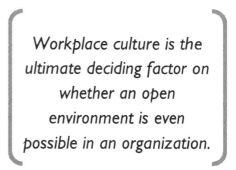

Workplace culture is the ultimate deciding factor on whether an open environment is even possible in an organization.

Consider the case of Procter & Gamble (P&G). As we saw back in Chapter 5, since 2000, when A.G. Lafley became chief executive officer, the leaders of P&G have worked hard to instill a culture of innovation and make innovation part of the daily routine. They have successfully preserved P&G's core research and development capability and their cadre of world-class technologists who are masters of the core technologies critical to the household and personal-care businesses. At the same time, they have made the entire innovation process more open by bringing more P&G employees outside R&D into the innovation circle. With every change, they have strived to create an enterprise-wide social system that harnesses the skills and insights of people throughout, and even from outside, the company with one common focus: the consumer. P&G strongly believes that without a deeply ingrained culture of innovation, a strategy of sustainable growth and competitive advantage cannot be achieved and maintained.

In this chapter we will look at *three* techniques that can help organizations instill a culture of innovation in their environment:

1. Gauging Organizational Commitment
2. Recognizing That Actions Speak Louder Than Words
3. Articulating a Clear Innovation Strategy

Gauging Organizational Commitment

Figuring out the level of commitment to innovation your organization truly has is ultimately where the rubber meets the road. While every organization is different, here are six questions that can help gauge organizational commitment.

✓ Is there a clear definition of success?

✓ Are identified resources available for success?

✓ Will resources be able to support innovation initiatives so that results are timely and relevant?

✓ What logistical support will be available to support an innovative environment?

✓ Are appropriate recognition programs in place to encourage innovation?

✓ Are incentives aligned to favor operational efficiency over innovation?

Regardless of how uncomfortable these seemingly simple questions might make your organization, they must be answered for any innovation program to be of true value and create a sustainable competitive advantage.

Consider the first question of what defines success. Is success defined by the:

- ✓ Number of ideas?
- ✓ Number of people involved?
- ✓ Total amount of money spent?
- ✓ Cost savings?
- ✓ Return on Investment (ROI), and if so, how do you calculate it?
- ✓ Number of Research & Development (R&D) efforts?
- ✓ Number of new products or services introduced over a given period of time?
- ✓ Percentage of revenue from new products and services?
- ✓ "Time to market" starting from the initial idea to the launch of a new product or service?
- ✓ A combination of two or more of the above?

As you can see, not only are there are a number of criteria that can affect what might constitute success, but each key stakeholder might have a completely different opinion on which criteria are more important. For an innovation program to be successful it is absolutely critical that all key stakeholders agree upon the exact definition of success and how success will be measured (see the Side Box "The First Mover Advantage Fallacy" on page 84).

Once success is defined, the next question is whether your organization has the necessary resources and logistical support identified and committed to achieve the desired outcomes in a timely and relevant manner. We saw in Principle 2 (Innovation Is a Journey, Not a Destination) that organizations are not really designed for innovation; they are designed for efficiencies. To overcome that impediment, your organizational incentives and recognition programs must be purposefully designed to encourage innovation rather than simply favoring operational efficiencies and cost saving efforts.

The First Mover Advantage Fallacy
Continued

The second challenge stems from first movers often falling into trap of thinking that "they know best" since their initial idea helped the customer satisfy a previously unmet need. However, as customers use a product or service and become more familiar with its features, their needs invariably change. Therefore, first movers must also continuously adapt their innovative product or service to suit the changing needs of their customers.

Many pundits have pontificated on the reasons behind TiVo's failure to capitalize on its first mover status. Invariably, the gist boils down to two factors: not creating a high enough barrier to entry and not understanding what their consumers really wanted to do.

A 2009 article in *The Economist*, "The Revolution That Wasn't," summarizes the problem as, "Just because technology enables people to do something does not mean they will, particularly when it comes to a medium as indolence-inducing as television" (The Economist, 2009). Although early adopters of DVRs used them a lot since they paid so much for them, later adopters used them much less. TiVo, however, kept adding features to allow TV watchers to create dynamic viewing experiences. That is simply not the "job" most people are trying to accomplish when they watch television. In the meantime, generic DVRs were coming out with a much reduced feature set (and therefore learning curve), which mapped perfectly to the "job" that most television watchers want to do (which is to have fun and be entertained). In other words, TiVo is a perfect example of a company that fell prey to the classic *customer centric paradox* discussed in Chapter 1.

Think about popular innovative products that you use today. Examples include search engines such as Google or Bing, e-commerce sites such as eBay or Amazon, and devices such as an iPad or iPhone. How many of these products were first in the markets in which they lead today?

Recognizing That Actions Speak Louder Than Words

As a leader, just talking about innovation is not enough. This is especially true if all you reward is execution at the end of the day. In fact, doing so is a surefire way to stifle innovation since your actions strongly suggest that execution is where employees should be focusing their attention.

The importance of senior leadership involvement and commitment for successful innovation is obvious when you look at some of the world's most innovative companies such as Amazon (Jeff Bezos), P&G (A.G. Lafley), and Salesforce.com (Marc Benioff).

A key reason why these companies are successful innovators year after year can be directly traced to the hands-on approach to innovation adopted by their respective senior leaders.

> *Leaders who value innovation realize that the buck stops with them.*

Conversely, leaders in companies that are less successful with innovation do not feel personally responsible for driving innovation in their organization. Rather, these leaders only see themselves as facilitators and leave the real work of driving innovation to someone else.

In his latest book, *The Innovator's DNA*, Clayton Christensen and his two coauthors present many examples of companies that exhibit what he refers to as an "innovation premium" (Dyer, Gregersen, & Christensen, 2011). They define innovation premium as "the portion of a company's market value that cannot be accounted for from the net present value of cash flows of its current products in its current markets." In other words, it's the premium that investors put on a company because they believe the company will launch new offerings and enter new markets that will generate even larger income streams that what it has today.

Their research shows that this innovation premium can be directly attributed to the company's senior leaders, specifically the chief executive officer. One of Christensen's examples is Apple's performance under Steve Jobs. Apple's innovation premium during Jobs' first tenure at Apple from

1980–1985 was 37%. A key reason for this was that Jobs was personally involved in innovation. We saw one such example in Principle 1 (Innovation Is One Percent Ideation and Ninety-Nine Percent Implementation) where Jobs got key ideas for the Macintosh computer (mouse and GUI) during his visit to Xerox PARC. Xerox meanwhile, as we saw in Chapter 2, has the dubious honor of being the company that snatched one of the greatest defeats from the jaws of victory!

Do you remember what happened at Apple during Jobs' hiatus from 1985–1998? According to the authors, Apple's innovation premium plummeted to an average of 30 percent because investors lost confidence in its ability to innovate and grow. After Jobs returned, Apple's innovation premium jumped to a whopping 52 percent. In fact, for a few a moments on an afternoon in August 2011, Apple overtook Exxon as the most valuable company in America, with a valuation of $1.5 billion more than that of Exxon! The mere fact that Apple could challenge Exxon is not a testimony to Americans' love affair with personal electronics but more so with those companies that have an ability to innovate.

There's another benefit to innovative leaders: they sow the seeds for the next generation of innovative companies. This is evident from the numerous star engineers who have left Apple to start their own mobile companies. Apple alumni not only benefit themselves, they contribute to the overall economy by creating new jobs and to Apple by creating more mobile apps for its AppStore ecosystem.

Another example that the authors discuss is that of P&G, which had an innovation premium of 23 percent from 1985–2000 before A.G. Lafley became CEO. Lafley's hands-on approach and commitment to innovation have boosted the company's innovation premium to 35 percent.

The lesson is that executives who value innovation realize that the buck stops with them. Rather than pointing fingers at others, they exemplify the behavior and commitment to innovation themselves.

Tarak believes that innovation is everyone's job in our globally competitive economy. For innovation to successfully be of real value (and contribute to the bottom line), Tarak shows us that ideas must be followed up with implementation. In Part 1 of his book, *Living in the Innovation Age*, Tarak helps us understand that the ultimate goal of innovation is to create a sustainable competitive advantage. He discusses how, in order to remain competitive, the product or service must provide real value to the consumer, be differentiated from competitors' offerings, and present a significant barrier to imitation.

In Part 2, Tarak introduces five principles that can help organizations prosper in this fundamentally unique era. As he explains, innovation is about creating the future, through visioning and action. I believe successfully applying this concept has driven growth at CALIBRE. In Part 3, Tarak discusses how one can implement innovation in their organization. He presents three techniques that he has applied in his professional career and that have been shown to spur innovation. Finally, in Part 4, Tarak provides an overview of the typical innovation lifecycle from ideation to execution and leaves his readers with a practical, ready-to-use maturity model, which they can use to lead their organizations to their desired stage of innovation maturity.

Throughout his book, Tarak cuts through the status quo of conventional thinking, and walks us through the process that a company must take to innovate and realize its "next big thing." He explains that innovation is not just about introducing something new, it literally means a process that renews something that exists, and effective innovation is more about the implementation of an idea than the idea itself.

Charles Darwin once said that, "It is not the strongest of the species that survive, or the most intelligent, but the one most responsive to change." As Tarak explains, despite creativity and technical expertise, companies fail when they do not embrace innovation and focus on implementation, converting ideas into reality. Innovation is a journey and the road to successful innovation may have struggles along the way; failures are just milestones along this long journey to success. As he further elaborates, living and prospering in this innovation age is neither an option nor a luxury, but an absolute necessity for survival in today's extremely competitive and global

novation Strategy

ful company without a corporate level hort is in their failure to develop and ation strategy.

ssical management, which focuses on esent with optimal efficiency. But ation, however, focus on three areas: go of the past, and creating the future n, 2006).

and managing the present are two trategy is an essential component of esonates from the top down. An the overall corporate strategy with fy innovation as a strategic initiative nnovation is aligned with corporate

can help answer the following

what are their true needs? ou really have? e tension? competencies and strengths to ate? ages and how can you maintain

he things that keep you awake at

ng Organizational Commitment), s so simple. For example, take a mary customer?" and consider

McDonald's, which has over 32,000 restaurants and more than 58 million customers each day. Who is McDonald's primary customer?

Of course, you and me, and anyone who eats their burgers, right?

However, in the 1980s and 1990s, McDonald's considered its primary customers to be multisite real estate developers and franchise owners, and not the people who ate in its restaurants. This marketing approach allowed McDonald's to focus most of its resources on its primary customers through centralized real estate development, franchising, and procurement functions. This strategy worked, and McDonald's opened 1,700 new stores each year during the 80s and 90s.

> Defining the primary customer is absolutely critical to successful innovation.

However, in 2003 the new chief executive officer, Jim Cantalupo, realized that the definition of the primary customer had to change. And McDonald's primary customer became the people eating at their restaurants.

That decision had profound implications in the way McDonald's did resource allocation. McDonald's reallocated resources from centralized corporate functions to regional managers, who were encouraged to customize local menus and store amenities to suit local tastes. Until 2003, McDonald's had a fairly common menu worldwide. It now serves breakfast porridge in the United Kingdom, soup in Portugal, and burgers that are topped with French cheese in France.

Defining the primary customer is absolutely critical to successful innovation. Let's say your primary customer values low cost. It's probably not in your best interest to innovate by adding new features that will raise the price of your service or product.

Another crucial question is around generating enough creative tension to spur innovation. Many highly innovative organizations rank their employees on the basis of their demonstrated performance. These rankings affect who is promoted, who is placed on probation, and who is asked to leave. General Electric's Jack Welch was famous for this approach. Nike's chief executive officer, Mark Parker, is known for generating creative tension by firing up friendly rivalries between divisions by posting each division's results. Obviously, each approach has pros and cons. One challenge, of course, is to prevent the competition from becoming negative and destructive. We'll explore this in more detail in our next chapter.

The Bottom Line

✓ True innovation requires organizational commitment to a culture shift away from just emphasizing efficiencies and near-term results.

✓ Innovation cannot be an afterthought. It must be well thought out and articulated with a corporate level innovation strategy.

✓ Senior leaders are as responsible – if not more – for ensuring real innovation occurs by showing it in their actions and not just their words.

8

Leveraging the Medici Effect

The Renaissance Age, spanning between the 14th and 17th centuries, was a cultural movement during which literature, science, art, religion, and politics thrived. There is a general consensus that the Renaissance Age began in Florence, Tuscany in the 14th century. However, there are varying theories on its origins with the most popular being the patronage of Florence's dominant family, the Medici.

Historians who back this theory contend that the Medici family acted as the catalyst for innovation during the Renaissance by bringing together people from vastly different professions and cultural backgrounds. This enabled a unique exchange and confluence of ideas that had never before been possible.

Organizations can leverage the Medici effect by providing an environment that encourages the free exchange of ideas and promotes collaboration.

California's Silicon Valley, a hub for entrepreneurship and innovation, is often considered a modern example of the Medici effect because many credit its success to the cultural diversity in a small concentrated area.

Organizations, too, can leverage the Medici effect by providing a safe and unencumbered environment that encourages the free exchange of ideas and promotes collaboration between people with different skills, competencies, and backgrounds.

In this chapter we will look at *four* techniques that can help organizations leverage the Medici effect to spur innovation in their environment:

1. Rethinking Workspace Design
2. Harnessing the Community
3. Collecting Ideas from Everyone and Everywhere
4. Making Innovation a Team Sport

Rethinking Workspace Design

Franklin Becker once said that organizations and employees perform either better or worse because of the way their workspaces are planned, designed, and managed. Scott Adams has made a fortune by mocking bland, dreary, and bureaucratic workplaces in his Dilbert cartoons.

The question is, should we be surprised at how our organizations have evolved over the years? The answer to this question is obvious once you consider the fact that professional management was born from the desire to optimize and control, not lead waves of change. In fact, the fathers of scientific management Fredrick Taylor, Henry Ford, and Henry Gantt are famous for making our work as boring as possible. They strived to remove all variability from work, minimize chance, and take away individual control and decisions.

One reason innovative companies succeed is because they realize the disconnect between how traditional organizations are designed and what is really required for innovation to occur. They realize that enabling collaborative workspaces internally, on campus grounds, and virtually can unlock areas for workers to be inspired, socially energized, and refreshed.

For example, Procter & Gamble has created a 10,000 square foot innovation center called the gym. It's an "on-site" off-site that is designed to stimulate innovation with an open design, easily moveable furniture, lots of low tech surfaces to write on, a café, and modern information display technology.

Mattel also has a similar on-campus off-site as part of Project Platypus where 12 employees with different skills and backgrounds conceive and develop new brands. For three months these teams leave their jobs and their titles behind and live in a separate 2,000 square foot building that looks more like a playground than a workplace.

Google also has been largely recognized for its fun and stimulating environment through the use of color, lighting, design, and music. Designing a workplace that's deliberately irreverent, playful, innovative, and reflects the Google brand has not only helped them attract and retain 'innovative' people but has made them one of the most sought after companies to work for.

> *Innovative companies succeed because they realize the disconnect between traditional organization design and what is really required for innovation to occur.*

Does this mean your workspace has to be exactly like that of one of companies above? No, but it does mean that your workspace needs to reflect the innovative culture that you are trying to instill. Your workplace design is not only a means of demonstrating this culture, but also a way to breed and strengthen the execution and delivery of innovative ideas and their implementation.

Harnessing the Community

If, as we talked about in Principle 4 (Innovation Seeks to Be Free), innovation thrives in an environment that is open, participatory, and collaborative, then it follows that innovation requires a strong and thriving community.

One approach to building that community is by leveraging the concept of Town Hall meetings. Robert Benmosche, chairman of MetLife, is a big fan of town hall meetings. He holds them frequently and considers them investments in creating tangible returns in the future. I recently met a senior technology executive who used this very concept to foster a strong community of her technology professionals. Her organization, not unlike most others, is organized by business domains, which are functional groups consisting of deep subject matter experts. These business domains also included technology professionals from various disciplines. This is a challenge many of us would face in a similar situation: "how do these technology professionals bond together, communicate, and exchange ideas to improve their productivity and foster innovation?" That's what led her to the institute quarterly Town Hall meetings for these technology professionals spread across the organizations. These town halls, which have been quite successful in promoting a culture of trust, collaboration, and innovation, are events that are organized by the technology community, for the technology community, and of the technology community.

Collecting Ideas from Everyone and Everywhere

Linus Pauling says, "the only way to have a good idea is to have lots of ideas." Now here's a guy who is well qualified to give us advice on how to have good ideas. After all, he's had two Nobel prizes (Nobelprize.org)!

To make sure that her organization generates and captures all ideas, the senior technology executive I mentioned above went beyond instituting town hall meetings. She provided a safe and readily available venue for raising and discussing new ideas. This ideas portal allows anyone to contribute an idea. Submitted ideas are discussed, "liked" and "disliked," and voted on for "popularity." Periodically, the top ideas compete before the business domains. Essentially she has created an open, participatory, and transparent community that naturally enforces the "survival of the fittest" for ideas (see the Side Box "Overcoming Idea Killers" on page 97).

As we saw in Principle 4 (Innovation Seeks to Be Free), the concept of an ideas portal or market is well tested and has proven to be an excellent tool to promote, spur, and democratize innovation beyond a limited few.

Overcoming Idea Killers

As you might have realized by now, real creation is unlike the stories that you may have heard about the epiphanies of technology legends. On the contrary, real creation is just plain old sloppy. We saw in Principles 1 and 2 that having an idea is just the beginning of a long road ahead. For an idea to have a chance of success, the organization must overcome many idea killers. Have you ever had a really good idea only to see people all over trying to squash your enthusiasm with statements such as the following?

- ✗ "We don't have a problem."
- ✗ "We've been successful, why change?"
- ✗ "Are you're saying we've failed?"
- ✗ "What's your hidden agenda?"
- ✗ "No one else does this!"
- ✗ "Tried it before – didn't work."
- ✗ "Too difficult," "Not the right time," "Too much work."

John Kotter, the author of many books including *Leading Change* and *Our Iceberg Is Melting*, classifies these attacks into four categories (Kotter, 2010): *Character assassination, Confusion, Death by delay,* and *Fear mongering*.

Overcoming Idea Killers
Continued

All of us have probably experienced these attacks first hand. Maybe some of us have used these attacks on someone else. **The best, and perhaps only, way to overcome these attacks is to anticipate them and have well-prepared responses in your back pocket.**

One attack type I find particularly interesting is the Devil's Advocate Attack. In this attack, the attacker invokes the "devil" and attacks not only your idea, but sometimes, you personally as well. Worse yet, the attacker is totally immune to any repercussions since it's not really them, but the "devil" that is making them say these things!

As we saw in "Collecting Ideas from Everyone and Everywhere," recently many companies have been launching innovation "centers" to ensure that innovative ideas are not squashed before they ever see a ray of daylight. One key reason why the senior technology executive I mentioned in my example was successful in launching an "ideas portal" in her organization was that she had anticipated the common "tried it before – didn't work" idea killer. She proactively made sure that the ideas portal was presented as being business-driven, collaborative, and operationally-focused. Furthermore, the connection with "reality" was reinforced by having senior leadership from the organization's business domains sponsor the innovation center. This reinforcement provided her another critical benefit as well – it continues to ensure that the innovation center does not just promote ideation but encourages follow through with implementation, which, as we saw in Principle I (Innovation is one percent ideation and 99 percent implementation), is the key to converting good ideas into great products.

Two examples we discussed back in Chapter 5 were Starbucks and Dell. Another company that successfully used this concept to promote innovation is the parent of Taco Bell, KFC, and Pizza Hut, Yum! Brands (Carlson, 2011).

A multi-national company, Yum! Brands has 38,000 restaurants and more than one million employees and associates around the world. Yum! Brands is leveraging its diverse base of employees and associates by providing them with an advanced messaging and collaboration system called iCHING where they share and exchange ideas and best practices around the clock and around the globe. The company's vice president of IT, Dickie Oliver, is a key proponent of iCHING and believes that the collaborative culture that has emerged has had a significant positive impact on innovation. For example, the KFC Team in Australia shared some of its product development insights on iCHING that led others within Yum! Brands to introduce an Australian beverage line called Krushers in their own markets. Another example includes a team in the United Kingdom taking a few tips from the success of Taco Bell's Crunchwrap Supreme and coming up with a similar offering.

Making Innovation a Team Sport

Principle 1 states that innovation is 99 percent implementation. That means, it is one thing to have great ideas but implementing them is a completely different ball game. When most people think of innovation, they immediately think of "bat caves" and "skunkworks" types of highly secretive and covert organizations. Yet, research has shown that the most innovative companies treat innovation as a "team sport" in which they not only involve their "R&D" folks but also members from marketing, sales, business development, and operations.

Granted, there are several examples of successful skunkworks based innovation. The U-2 and SR-71 Blackbird high-altitude spy planes are masterpieces of aeronautical engineering and products of the very first skunkworks that Kelly Johnson created at Lockheed.

Figure 11: Innovation is a team sport.

IBM's first, and highly profitable, PC came out of a Big Blue skunkworks initiative in Boca Raton, Florida. And Steve Jobs ran Apple's breakthrough Macintosh computer as a renegade skunkworks that ultimately annihilated its Apple II internal rival. But these examples are the exception and not the norm as most skunkworks initiatives barely make it out of the lab and if they do, they die a slow and miserable death before they ever make it to the market.

So, what's wrong with the skunkworks model?

First of all, consider the management message that you are sending when you create a skunkworks within your organization. You're basically saying there are two classes of employees – the chosen few who are believed to have the ability (and smarts) to innovate and the rest of the non-innovative, unimaginative, and less creative employees. A skunkworks may occasionally give birth to great new ideas, but it almost always breeds even greater resentment within the organization. The skunkworks is seen as an "elite" organization that receives special treatment and an unfair amount of opportunities at the expense of the rest of the organization.

Most skunkworks are actually management "cries for help" in disguise. What management is really saying, sometimes without even knowing it, is that they have failed to create an organization that can innovate. Setting up a skunkworks is simply the easiest thing to do. It is easy to find talented people who want to work hard, do new things, and come up with ideas as a full-time job.

> *The entire innovation process from ideas to implementation must be democratized.*

By creating a skunkworks, management has just taken the easy way out by offloading the responsibility for innovation to one group in the company. They feel good that they now have "one throat to hug and one throat to choke."

Ultimately, most skunkworks never live up to their expectations primarily because of the resentment they face from the rest of the organization and the resulting lack of support from critical parts of the company such as productions/operations, marketing, etc. Govindrajan and Trimble in their book, *The Other Side of Innovation*, refer to operations as the 800 pound gorilla (Govindarajan & Trimble, 2010). Without their support, any idea that comes out of skunkworks has a very slim chance of succeeding.

A better set up for success is making sure innovation is presented as a team sport (Figure 11) from the very beginning. Not only do ideas come from everywhere and everybody, but all employees are responsible for and empowered to implement the selected ideas as well. Having all parts of the organization involved in the implementation from the very beginning helps the innovation accomplish two key transitions that are critical for success – the transition of the idea to implementation within the organization and the transition of the implementation to a product or service within the market.

Organizational transition of an idea to implementation requires that the majority of the organization buys into the premise of the idea and provide meaningful support to the idea by helping it integrate within the organization's production cycle, financial cycle, and sales and marketing cycles. As discussed above, most skunkworks are resented by the rest of the organization thus immediately putting them at a disadvantage regardless of how much potential their ideas and prototypes have. In fact, an internal study conducted by American Express in the late 1990s found that 85 percent of problems attributed to the failure of projects coming out of skunkworks were the result of not involving the right people from the beginning (Brown & Ulijn, 2004).

Two classic examples of organizations that chronically failed to transition implementation of ideas to profitable products in the market are Digital Research Inc. (DRI) and Xerox. As we saw in Principle 1 (Innovation Is One Percent Ideation and Ninety-Nine Percent Implementation) in Part 2, neither Microsoft nor Apple might have been the powerhouse they are today had Digital Research Inc. (DRI) and Xerox been more capable of transitioning their respective innovations to the market.

So, the moral is that not only should the process of soliciting ideas be democratized but the entire innovation process from ideas to implementation to product/service should be democratized. Cross functional teams with full organizational support guarantee the best chance of success for innovative ideas to thrive and make it to market.

The Bottom Line

✓ Innovative organizations attract other innovators by providing an environment that promotes the free exchange and confluence of ideas from different areas.

✓ Innovative ideas can come from anyone, anywhere, and anytime.

✓ Innovation thrives when everyone from across the company is involved in it from the very beginning. Conversely, innovation rarely succeeds in a "throw it over the wall" type environment.

9

Knowing What to Measure – Picking the Right Innovation Metrics

We've all heard the cliché, "You are what you eat." Not surprisingly, process experts have adapted this to, "You are what you measure."

Metrics, as measurements are called, provide us with an objective view of the state of a process or phenomenon. Metrics commonly collected by organizations include market share, sales increases, margins, and customer satisfaction. While there are many reasons to collect metrics, the

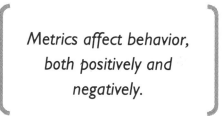

Metrics affect behavior, both positively and negatively.

ultimate purpose is best described in the saying, "If you can't measure it, you can't manage it" - a phrase that is widely attributed to a variety of renowned gurus from Peter Drucker to W. Edwards Deming to Tom DeMarco.

Metrics affect behavior, both positive and negative.

There's an interesting case study about NASCAR that illustrates the power of the effective use of metrics. NASCAR sponsors had long realized that the key to maximizing their revenue potential was to get the most spectators to come watch the races in order to maximize advertising revenue. Spectators in turn want to attend races that have the best and most drivers.

So in 1971, NASCAR redesigned what they measured to make sure that the most competitive drivers participated in the most races. Instead of the

When Good Metrics Go Bad
The Downside of Metrics

For over a century, 3M has produced a vast array of innovative products such as masking tape and Post-it® notes that are household names today. But even 3M is not immune to challenges in making sure that it continues to be an innovation leader. For years 3M prided itself on at least 33 percent of its sales from products released in the past five years. Today, 3M struggles to keep that level at 25 percent.

3M's troubles began more than a couple of decades ago, and by the late 1990s, everyone within the company and on Wall Street knew that something had to change if 3M was to ever recover to its past glory. In response, 3M's board named James McNerney of GE fame as the new CEO on December 5, 2000. Within days, 3M's stock jumped nearly 20%. McNerney was the first outsider to lead 3M in its 100-year history and as expected, within the first few months, McNerney made massive changes within 3M. He axed 8,000 workers (about 11% of the workforce), intensified the performance-review process, and emphasized strict operational efficiency.

Perhaps the biggest change he introduced was with GE's Six Sigma program with the goal of decreasing production defects and increasing efficiency.

When Good Metrics Go Bad
Continued

Wall Street loved his changes as 3M's lackluster stock jolted back to life and McNerney won accolades for bringing discipline to an organization that had become inefficient and sluggish (Hindo, 2007).

Innovation at 3M, however, did not come back. Traditionally, 3M had always been a place where researchers were given wide latitude to pursue research and spend years testing products. Consider, for example, the Post-it note. Its inventor, Art Fry, and others, tinkered with the idea for several years before the product went into full production in 1980.

With Six Sigma, a rigorous statistical analysis-based process was laid over the phase-review process for innovations. The goal was to speed up the progression of ideas to the new-product pipeline, almost to the point of having something that would produce a profit within a couple of quarters of the idea being introduced! So, why did innovation suffer and is it merely a coincidence?

Experts agree that the drop in innovation was not surprising. Efficiency programs such as Six Sigma are designed to reduce variation and eliminate defects. But these types of initiatives can have an adverse effect on creativity and innovation, both of which thrive in an environment where failure and risk taking are tolerated, encouraged, and even celebrated. 3M's current CEO says, "Invention is by its very nature a disorderly process," and has cut back many of McNerney's innovation initiatives. Interestingly, early in the Six Sigma effort, after a meeting at which technical employees were briefed on the new process, they concluded that it would have been impossible for anything like a Post-it note to have ever emerged from the new system. There is no doubt that Six Sigma works well in a production environment where the outcomes are well defined. But as we discussed in Principle 3 (Innovation Is "Where No Man Has Gone Before"), innovation is about where no one has gone before, meaning there are few facts to go on and the outcomes are fuzzy at best.

When Good Metrics Go Bad
Continued

MIT Sloan School of Management professor Eric Von Hippel, who has worked with 3M on several innovation projects, is familiar with what happened at 3M. His project got put on the backseat in a situation that he summarized as, "New things look very bad on this scale." Govindrajan, author of *The Other Side of Innovation* and management professor at Dartmouth's Tuck School of Business has summarized what happened at 3M as, "The more you hardwire a company on total quality management, [the more] it is going to hurt breakthrough innovation. The mindset that is needed, the capabilities that are needed, the metrics that are needed, the whole culture that is needed for discontinuous innovation, are fundamentally different."

Errors are the lifeblood of innovation. History is full of examples of innovations that were the result of accidents and errors. Alexander Flemming discovered the virtues of penicillin when mold accidentally contaminated a culture of Staphylococcus he had left by an open window in his lab. Think of how many lives have been saved because of that one accident. Modern electronics owe their existence to a few errors as well, a few of which ultimately led to the creation of the vacuum tube! In fact, it is said that when Lee De Forest first invented the vacuum tube even he did not completely understand why it worked! Now, how is that for Six Sigma?

On the other hand, total R&D budget seems like a reasonable metric. After all, the more a company spends on R&D, the more innovative it is likely to be. But then, how does one explain the fact that according to the 2010 Global Innovation 1000 study of corporate innovation spending performed by the management consulting firm Booz Allen Hamilton (BAH), the three most innovative companies of our time – Apple, Google, and 3M – were not even part of the top 40 biggest research and development spenders

(Jaruzelski & Dehoff, 2010)? In fact, of the top 10 biggest spenders, only three are in the top 10 most innovative companies.

Excessive resources, budget or headcount, might actually result in lowered due diligence and less rigorous analysis. Another metric is counting the number of ideas submitted, but simply measuring the number of ideas might lead to the same idea being submitted in different forms or ideas merely being submitted for the sake of submission.

Percentage of sales from new products or services seems reasonable except when you consider the fact that this could lead to either incremental innovation on existing products or services or cannibalization of existing products or services in favor of new ones to meet a sales target.

On the other end of the spectrum is metrics overload caused by having too many metrics. When an organization has too many metrics that try to measure everything, often the result is that nothing really gets measured. There is just too much

> *Determining the right metrics is not only a question of "how many." It's also a question of "which ones."*

data to separate the proverbial "wheat from the chaff." Too many metrics leads to excessive activities that provide little value, cause confusion, and could even result in conflicting behavior.

As an example, Figure 12 illustrates a typical airplane cockpit. What if the dashboard of your car looked like that? Can you imagine having to constantly evaluate so many gauges while driving at 100+ mph on the German Autobahn? While having so many "metrics" might make sense in an airplane cockpit, the same does not apply to the dashboard of your car. Commercial airline pilots receive hundreds of hours of training before they can fly a plane. As a result of their rigorous training, pilots understand each and every "metric" and how it affects their flight. Conversely, most car drivers receive almost no training at all. Providing car drivers with too many metrics about the car on their dashboard would only confuse them with potentially deadly consequences.

Figure 12: A typical airplane cockpit.

Determining the right metrics is not only a question of "how many." It's also a question of "which ones." Figuring out which combination of metrics provides the most insight into your organization's innovation capability is as important as figuring out how many metrics to track.

Not picking the right combination can lead to what is referred to by many as "rear-view mirror" management. No one would ever even dream of driving a car solely looking in the rear-view mirror, would they? Yet, that's exactly what many organizations do when they pick only "backward looking" metrics. These include all measurements that are taken after the fact and include popular financial metrics such as ROI. The problem is that such metrics only tell you about what has already happened. As the popular saying in the stock trading world goes, "past performance is no indication of future returns." So while backwards looking metrics might help extrapolate the future, they really do not provide true insight. Forward looking metrics, on the other hand, can provide better insight into anticipating future outcomes and if necessary, proactively taking corrective action. Examples of such metrics include those associated with measuring the health of your innovation pipeline (see Chapter 11). In our car analogy, forward looking metrics are akin to driving while looking forward with a navigation system that charts the road ahead and helps avoid congestion/construction areas.

Ultimately, defining the right metrics for your innovation efforts is both an art and a science. It can especially be tricky since there is no single answer that is appropriate for every organization, which means that the optimal set of metrics will vary from company to company. Therefore, the best approach is to use a balanced mix of metrics that focus on the entire innovation lifecycle from inputs to outcomes. A typical innovation lifecycle with a few sample metrics for each phase is presented in the next chapter.

The Bottom Line

✓ Keep it simple by focusing on metrics that make sense to your environment.

✓ There are no magic metrics or silver bullets. The best approach is to use a balanced set of metrics that cover the entire innovation lifecycle.

✓ Imposing rigid processes with the goal of measuring everything could have an adverse effect of stifling your innovation initiatives.

Part 4

Embarking on Your Innovation Journey

There are many things you can do to spur innovation within your organization. To do so effectively requires answering two critical questions:

- ✓ Is there an end-to-end value chain for innovation?
- ✓ How do you know where to start and what to do first?

Chapter 10 addresses the first question with a discussion on the typical innovation lifecycle. The final chapter of this book, Chapter 11, addresses the second question by presenting a practical, ready-to-use innovation maturity model.

10

The Innovation Lifecycle

How do the most innovative companies continue to innovate while at the same time not being the biggest spenders on R&D? As we saw in the previous chapter, a study performed by Booz Allen Hamilton (BAH) revealed that the three most innovative companies of our time – Apple, Google, and 3M – were not even part of the top 40 biggest research and development spenders and, in fact, of the top 10 biggest spenders, only three were in the top 10 most innovative companies (Jaruzelski & Dehoff, 2010).

The previous chapter showed how imposing too much rigidity on innovation can stifle the very innovation it was meant to encourage. At the same time it seems intuitive that highly innovative companies can't succeed by allowing a "free-for-all" environment. Rather, these companies are successful because they have figured out the end-to-end value chain to commercialize their good ideas into successful products and services. This value chain is the Innovation Lifecycle and can be decomposed into six key stages:

1. **Ideation**

2. **Selection**

3. **Inception**

4. **Presentation**

5. **Elaboration**

6. **Transition**

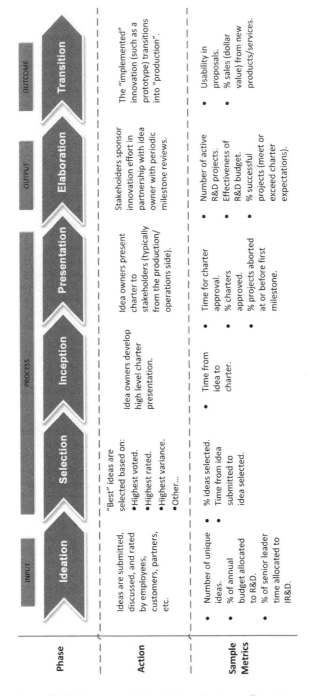

Figure 13: The Innovation Lifecycle from Ideation to Transition.

As shown in Figure 13, these stages are organized into four higher level categories: Inputs, Process, Outputs, and Outcomes. This lifecycle is independent of sector (public, private, or nonprofit), industry vertical, or company size. However, these factors as well as others such as organizational culture might result in varying degrees of formality across the lifecycle or even several stages being combined. In all cases, the essence of the lifecycle remains the same. Let's take a look at each of these four categories and six stages in more detail.

Innovation Inputs

Ideation

Ideation, which is the creative process of generating, developing, and communicating new ideas (Wikipedia), is a crucial part of the innovation lifecycle for it provides the necessary input for innovation to occur – a fertile ground of ideas. Despite the fact that innovation is only one percent ideation and 99% implementation (Principle 1), the fact remains that without an idea there would be nothing to implement.

> *A successful ideation environment provides a positive and constructive environment where all ideas can be discussed.*

The critical success factor for successful ideation is creating an open, collaborative, and safe environment, whether it is virtual, physical, or a combination of both, so that idea creators can submit ideas freely without fear of retribution or mockery.

For example, here are five simple rules that I communicate and enforce in ideation sessions:

Rule 1   *Respect all individuals, ideas, and time.*

Rule 2   *Have no fear.*

Rule 3   *Quantity is as important as quality.*

Rule 4   *Think out-of-the-box.*

Rule 5   *One team, one goal.*

At this point, all ideas should be accepted regardless of how they might appear. Most companies fail at this stage by prematurely judging the merit of an idea. A well-known example of this can be found in the story behind how FedEx came into existence. According to the story, in 1965, while future FedEx founder Frederick Smith was working on his Bachelor's degree in economics at Yale University, he outlined his concept for a profitable delivery service that would use a "hub and spokes" concept to handle the routing of parcels in a term paper for his economics class. Legend has it that the paper earned a poor grade and Smith took it on as a personal challenge to show the world that his idea had merit.

A successful ideation environment provides a positive and constructive environment where all ideas can be discussed and refined. Many environments provide a Facebook type "like" feature where participants can indicate their "support" of an idea by "liking" it. We discussed the concept of ideas portals in Chapter 8 in "Collecting Ideas from Everyone and Everywhere" and the Side Box "Overcoming Idea Killers" on page 97.

Innovation Process

Selection

Selection is the process in which the universe of ideas from the ideation phase is filtered down to a more manageable set to move forward. Exactly how this filtration happens is an art and a science that varies from organization to organization. The importance of this phase cannot be over emphasized since the effectiveness of this phase will impact how well an organization will be able to leverage its limited resources.

A typical trap that many organizations fall into at this phase is focusing too narrowly on Return on Investment (ROI). Clayton Christensen in *Innovation Killers: How Financial Tools Destroy Your Capacity to Do New Things,* describes in detail how standard business financial measures, such as ROI, used to evaluate investments creates a systematic bias against successful innovation (Christensen, Innovation Killers: How Financial Tools Destroy Your Capacity to Do New Things , 2010). Intuitively, it makes sense why ROI is not always the best metric for innovation.

> *A typical trap that many organizations fall into at this phase is focusing too narrowly on ROI.*

Think about this – if the ROI of an innovative idea could be determined with any level of predictability or confidence, wouldn't someone have already implemented it thereby no longer making it an innovation? Would anyone (including Jeff Bezos), even in their wildest dreams, have calculated the ROI of an idea of selling online books from a garage? And if they had, would Amazon ever have been created?

My guess is probably not. Better factors to consider at this stage might be how well the idea was received by others in ideation or even how much contention the idea created during ideation since that [contention] might be an indicator of just how disruptive the idea has the potential of being.

Inception

Inception is the phase where owners of "selected" ideas work through the questions about the feasibility of their ideas. At this point, the owners must make fundamental assumptions, anticipate challenges they might face, assess market maturity in terms of whether the idea could even be implemented and if so, whether customers are truly ready for their idea. As an example, consider YouTube, which within 16 months of its founding in February of 2005, was streaming 30 million videos a day!

Yes, a video-sharing website on which users can upload, share and view videos sounds like it would always be a sure hit. But would that really have been the case a decade ago? In the mid-1990s, almost every user connected to the Internet using dial-up 56K modems. A video that takes less than a few minutes to download today would have taken hours back then. Few consumers would have had the patience to use YouTube at those speeds.

In addition to today's high speed, ubiquitous broadband internet access, YouTube was

Inception focuses on the "feasibility" of an idea.

also able to leverage Adobe's Flash platform. YouTube may have never happened if its creators would have had to create a video standard from scratch. So, the idea of YouTube became a reality because the underpinnings (i.e., the maturity) to make it successful were already in existence (Johnson, 2010).

Presentation

Idea owners present their ideas during the Presentation phase. At this point, stakeholders who will ultimately decide which ideas will move forward with firm resource commitments should evaluate the feasibility of the proposals that are being presented.

For example, if the proposal has numbers or underlying assumptions, ensure that each one is properly grounded in reality. Consider whether the idea owner has adequately conducted due diligence with alternative analysis and multiple scenarios. Is the base case overly optimistic, or conversely, is the worst case bad enough? This is also the place to consider the financial questions around revenue and profitability. The final decision of which ideas to move forward should be based on an unbiased assessment of which ideas could:

✓ Sustain or provide a new competitive advantage for the organization.

✓ Surprise and delight customers by resetting their expectations either by providing them with a completely new and better way of doing what they can already do or meeting previously unmet needs.

✓ Create a completely new market or segment of customers.

Innovation Outputs

Elaboration

Elaboration has one ultimate goal – to maximize learning. Maximizing learning is about learning faster, better, and cheaper by testing ideas in a simulated real-world environment.

The ability to try out new ideas quickly and cheaply (i.e., efficiently) is an essential trait of all innovating companies. As we saw in Principle 2 (Innovation Is a Journey, Not a Destination), Google has an explicit philosophy of "innovation, not instant perfection" that allows Google to explore ideas by launching them early on Google Labs, iteratively learning what the market wants, and gradually taking the idea from "good to great."

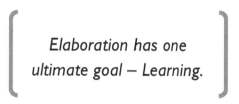

Elaboration has one ultimate goal – Learning.

P&G has a similar innovation motto, "Make a little, sell a little, learn a lot," which is why P&G often manufactures a small quantity of an experimental product, launches it in a test market, and learns a lot from the consumers' reactions.

According to Principle 2 (Innovation Is a Journey, Not a Destination), the key to successful experimentation is to seek the truth (i.e., verify the hypothesis) and not succumb to the pressures in organizations that push people toward interpretations of results that are comfortable and convenient rather than analytical and dispassionate. For successful innovation to happen these pressures must be understood and overcome.

Innovation Outcomes

Transition

In "Making Innovation a Team Sport," we saw that successful innovation requires two key transitions: the transition of the idea to implementation within the organization and the transition of the implementation to a product or service within the market.

Both transitions require that the majority of the organization buys into the premise of the idea and provides meaningful support to the idea by helping it integrate within the organization's production cycle, financial cycle, and sales and marketing cycles.

Planning for transition early on ensures that the innovation initiatives stay focused on the ultimate outcomes. Too often, people focus on process outputs. While outputs are important, they are not as important as process outcomes.

What is the difference? One of the better explanations is by Richard Hunter and George Westerman in *The Real Value of IT* (Hunter & Westerman, 2009) in which the authors ask their readers, "What is the value of an exercise machine?" What would you think if I answered using metrics such as how many hours the exercise machine (Figure 14) was used or the different levels of intensity it supports, the number of varying types of workouts it provides, or the residual value of the machine after depreciation? You probably would think these metrics aren't very useful.

Figure 14: What is the true value of an exercise machine?

But that, claim the authors, is exactly what most IT shops do when answering the question of what value they provide to the business. The problem is these metrics focus on outputs. Exercise machine users and business users of IT both care about outcomes. The real value of an exercise machine is in the ultimate outcome it helps achieve such helping its user lose weight, get in better shape, or get stronger. Most IT shops maintain a service level agreement (SLA) that guarantees minimum level of services to its business users. The problem with these SLAs is that they focus primarily on infrastructure "outputs" such as capacity utilization, server uptime, application response times, and

> *The real value of innovation to an organization is based on successful outcomes.*

network availability, rather than focusing on business outcomes such as revenue growth, customer retention, and cost reduction.

Similarly, the value of innovation to an organization is not measured by the number of ideas or the time taken for the ideas to be reviewed, filtered, and selected, or even in the number of R&D type projects it has going on. The real value of innovation to an organization is based on successful outcomes such as how much revenue and sales come from new products or services. These outcomes are in turn what directly contribute to the organization's sustained competitive advantage.

The Bottom Line

✓ Innovation thrives in an environment that encourages experimentation. Make sure your innovation lifecycle reflects this as well.

✓ An effective innovation lifecycle ensures that the most valuable ideas continue to move forward from initial concept to final production in a systematic and orderly manner.

✓ Recognize the difference between outputs and outcomes.

11

The Innovation Maturity Model

There are many things you can do to spur innovation within your organization. But how do you know where to start and what to do first?

This is a classic conundrum, perhaps best captured and conveyed in the story, "Alice in Wonderland." As Alice walks through Wonderland, she comes to an intersection in the road. Seeing her standing there befuddled, Cheshire Cat looks down from the tree above and says, "My dear, what's the problem?"

"There are so many roads to choose from. I don't know which way to go," she replies.

"Where are you going?" asks the Cheshire Cat.

"I have no idea," says Alice.

"Take any road you want," the Cat wisely answers. "If you don't know where you are going, any road will get you there!"

A successful innovation program requires a clear understanding of where you are today and where you want to be tomorrow.

The lesson is that implementing a successful innovation program requires a clear understanding of where you are today (current state) and where you want to be tomorrow (desired future state).

One tool that has been used with great success in the process improvement world to solve the above dilemma of "not knowing which road to take," is the maturity model. In simple terms, a maturity model is a structured collection of elements or attributes that describe the stages of maturity of an organization in a particular area.

A maturity model provides:

✓ A place to start, a place to end, and a roadmap of how to get there

✓ The benefit of a community's prior experiences

✓ A common language and a shared vision

✓ A framework for prioritizing actions

✓ A way to define what improvement means for your organization

✓ A standardized way to benchmark and compare different organizations

The process improvement community uses the Capability Maturity Model Integration® (CMMI). CMMI® was created by the Software Engineering Institute (SEI) in conjunction with both industry and government as a way for organizations to gauge their current process maturity and provide them a structured set of guidelines to help them move towards "better" processes (Software Engineering Institute).

The Innovation Maturity Model presented at Figure 15 has a similar intent. The model is organized along two dimensions - Traits and Maturity levels.

Innovation Maturity Model	Reactive	Constrained	Proactive		
			Open	Managed	Continuous
Culture	Risk Averse. Failure not accepted.	Managed risks are tolerated. Innovation is opaque outside limited R&D groups.	Risk taking is encouraged and ideas are encouraged.	Open, transparent, participatory, and collaborative.	Failure is celebrated. Innovation is recognized as a strategic, corporate initiative and a source of competitive advantage with full executive support.
Purpose	Survival.	Organic Growth.	Ensuring Customer and Market focus by using "outside" ideas and skills.	Building a robust portfolio of products and services.	Actively seeking disruption.
People	Individual Heroes.	R&D teams.	Idea Community.	Innovation Center.	Innovating Organization.
Processes	Lagging innovation in response to external factors - regulations, competitors, etc.	Basic innovation processes exist but innovation opportunities are restricted to specialized R&D groups. Processes lack maturity to move idea to implementation.	Innovation processes are defined, standardized, and institutionalized within the entire organization.	Innovation is managed quantitiatively via innovation pipeline and portfolio management. Quantitative Metrics are used to improve innovation processes.	Quantitative and qualitative metrics are used to continuously improve and optimize the Innovation processes.
Technology	None.	Internally focused.	Externally focused (idea mangement, collaboration, etc.).	Innovation pipeline management tools (similar to sales pipeline management). Idea Quality control.	Innovation dashboards.
Metrics	None.	R&D Budget. ROI.	Number of ideas submitted. % of senior leader time allocated to innovation.	Innovation Pipeline (ideas by phase and business area). Effectiveness of R&D budget. Process metrics (examples - Time from idea to charter, Time for charter approval, %age projects aborted at or before first milestone, %age successful projects i.e. meet or exceed charter expectations).	%age sales from new products & services, new customer segments, and new markets.

Figure 15: The Innovation Maturity Model is a useful tool to guide organizations in their innovation journey.

127

Traits

The traits (Figure 16) are the six elements identified in the model's first column (Figure 15). These traits are not mutually exclusive. People, process, and technology form the three core pillars of any organization. Culture represents the interaction between people and the how, what, and why of the processes. Purpose is identified by the how, what, and why people use technology. Finally, metrics represent the tangibles and intangibles of the processes and technologies that exist within the organization. Each of these six traits contributes to the maturity level of an organization and figuring out the maturity level of an organization requires analyzing each of these traits.

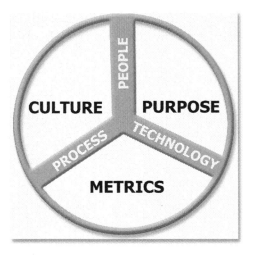

Figure 16: Each of the Six Maturity Model Traits contributes to the overall innovation maturity of an organization.

Maturity Levels

The two primary and four secondary innovation maturity levels are across the top row of the model (Figure 15). At the highest level, an organization is either reactive or proactive in its approach to innovation.

A Reactive Innovation organization is one where innovation is not recognized as a value-driving asset in the organization. The organization does not anticipate the need to evolve its products and service through innovation in a planned

> *Reactive Innovation does not recognize innovation as a value-driving asset.*

way, but instead waits for the evidence of the market to tell it, after the fact, where they need to adapt. Acting under the pressure of responding to a business challenge, the organization gravitates toward quick fixes rather than considering the true nature of the problem.

Organizations at this maturity level do not actively seek out ideas, but wait for a good idea to be presented. The classic reactive innovation technique is, at best, a suggestion box or an email address and at worse the proverbial "circular bin." The reactive innovation strategy is used by companies that are followers and have a focus on operations, a wait and see approach, and are only interested in low-risk opportunities. Since these companies are highly risk averse and do not tolerate failure well, their *modus operandi* is to copy proven innovation. As a result, these companies are in a continual survival mode. Companies with reactive innovation strategies include budget airlines such as Ryan Air, which has successfully copied the no-frills service model of Southwest Airlines (see Chapter 6, Business Model Innovation, for more information).

In contrast, the Proactive Innovation organization is one where innovation is viewed as a key discipline that must be fostered. In these organizations, innovation best practices have been identified and are in active deployment. Such organizations actively manage their innovation agenda, look for new opportunities and understand the intersection of its capabilities with the objectives of its current and future customers. These organizations provide their employees and partners with the tools and systems to accelerate and focus ideation efforts in support of a common innovation vision.

Proactive organizations take control of their destiny rather than waiting for their competitors to define their role for them. Proactive innovation is an approach that constantly and actively seeks to find great ideas and sponsor them. Proactive innovation means that the company constantly identifies new opportunities and challenges, and brainstorms ways to attempt to create new products and services.

> *Proactive Innovation views innovation as a key discipline that must be fostered.*

Companies with proactive innovation strategies tend to have strong research orientation; they will *often* have first mover advantage[2] and be a technology market leader. These companies access knowledge from a broad range of sources and take big bets/high risks. All companies that we have discussed in this book including 3M, Procter & Gamble, and Google and others such as DuPont, Apple, and Singapore Airlines have proactive innovation strategies.

Proactive innovation has four secondary maturity levels: constrained, open, managed, and continuous.

The Constrained Maturity Level

Constrained innovation is the most rudimentary form of Proactive Innovation. The culture in such an organization has shifted to accept carefully managed risks and almost all of the innovation occurs within cherry picked research and development (R&D) teams. The organization has basic innovation processes but lacks the maturity to move from a great idea to a successful implementation. Success is typically measured in terms of the R&D

---

[2] "Often" is italicized because as we discussed in Chapter 7, The First Mover Advantage Fallacy, first movement does not guarantee continued success. Furthermore, sustaining the first mover advantage and ensuring that it results in a profitable business is much more difficult.

budget and return on investment, both of which, as we saw in Chapter 9, are less than adequate measures of innovation.

The Open Maturity Level

At this level, innovation starts to become outward facing with the focus squarely on the customer and the market. The organizational culture is more accepting of leveraging outside ideas and skills. The culture has also evolved into one where risk taking is encouraged and ideas are openly accepted. Innovation processes for idea generation, evaluation, prioritization, and implementation are defined, standardized, and institutionalized within the entire organization. The organization makes widespread use of technologies for generating, sharing and collaborating on ideas. Innovation, at this stage of maturity, is no longer just limited to specialized R&D teams but can be taken on by any employee. Metrics for innovation are focused on inputs such as the number of ideas generated and percent of senior time spent on innovation related activities.

The Managed Maturity Level

At this level, the concepts of openness, collaboration, transparency, and participation of Principle 4 (Innovation Seeks to Be Free) become obvious. The organization's focus clearly shifts from organic growth to building a robust, future-resistant pipeline of products and services. Innovation is seen as a core competency and is managed quantitatively via innovation pipeline and portfolio management.

Technology enablement includes innovation pipeline management tools that assist senior leaders in systematically managing their innovation pipeline similar to what sales professionals have done for years with their sales pipeline. Metrics shift from being input-focused to metrics that are more process-focused. Examples include metrics based on a quantitative analysis of the innovation pipeline (ideas by phase and business area) and the measurement of effectiveness of the R&D budget. Process-based metrics also could be based on a variety of throughput-based metrics such as time from idea to charter, time for charter approval, percentage projects aborted at or before first milestone, and percentage of successful projects (i.e., meet or exceed charter expectations).

The Continuous Maturity Level

In the continuous maturity level, the organizational culture fully embraces innovation during this nirvana stage of maturity. Organizations at this level actively seek disruption and opportunities to venture into new and unchartered waters. The culture shifts from one where risk is avoided to one where failure is celebrated and seen as a learning opportunity. Innovation is recognized as a strategic, corporate initiative and a source of competitive advantage with full executive support.

Innovation metrics are output and outcome based with both quantitative and qualitative metrics such as percentage of sales from new products and services, new customer segments, and new markets being used to continuously improve and optimize the innovation processes. Senior leaders are actively engaged in innovation, and innovation and creativity is ingrained in the organization's core values.

Applying the Innovation Maturity Model

As stated earlier in the chapter, the primary purpose of a maturity model is to help organizations gauge their current maturity and provide them a structured set of guidelines that can help them move towards their desired level of maturity.

To see the Innovation Maturity Model in action, let's say an organization claims it wants to build out and maintain a robust pipeline of products and services to sustain its competitiveness in the market. The organization has a dedicated R&D team responsible for coming up with new offerings. The R&D team is allocated a fixed budget (percentage of revenue goal) each year and is seen as a cost center.

Since the organization is dispersed across multiple geographic locations, its workforce is used to using collaborative technologies. Figure 17 shows this scenario mapped on the model with yellow shading indicating that the organization is primarily operating at the Constrained Innovation Maturity

Innovation Maturity Model	Reactive	Proactive			
		Constrained	Open	Managed	Continuous
Culture	Risk Averse. Failure not accepted.	Managed risks are tolerated. Innovation is opaque outside limited R&D groups.	Risk taking is encouraged and ideas are encouraged.	Open, transparent, participatory, and collaborative.	Failure is celebrated. Innovation is recognized as a strategic, corporate initiative and a source of competitive advantage with full executive support.
Purpose	Survival.	Organic Growth.	Ensuring Customer and Market focus by using "outside" ideas and skills.	Building a robust portfolio of products and services.	Actively seeking disruption.
People	Individual Heroes.	R&D teams.	Idea Community.	Innovation Center.	Innovating Organization.
Processes	Lagging innovation in response to external factors - regulations, competitors, etc.	Basic innovation processes exist but Innovation opportunities are restricted to specialized R&D groups. Processes lack maturity to move idea to implementation.	Innovation processes are defined, standardized, and institutionalized within the entire organization.	Innovation is managed quantitatively via innovation pipeline and portfolio management. Quantitative Metrics are used to improve innovation processes.	Quantitative and qualitative metrics are used to continuously improve and optimize the innovation processes.
Technology	None.	Internally focused.	Externally focused (Idea management, collaboration, etc.).	Innovation pipeline management tools (similar to sales pipeline management). Idea Quality control.	Innovation dashboards.
Metrics	None.	R&D Budget. ROI.	Number of ideas submitted. % of senior leader time allocated to innovation.	Innovation Pipeline (ideas by phase and business area). Effectiveness of R&D budget. Process metrics (examples - Time from idea to charter, Time for charter approval, %age projects aborted at or before first milestone, %age successful projects i.e. meet or exceed charter expectations).	%age sales from new products & services, new customer segments, and new markets.

Figure 17: The Innovation Maturity Model shaded to depict the current state of innovation within a fictitious organization.

level. Figuring out the current state is often easier said than done. A tool that can help is the Innovation Quotient Self-Assessment in Appendix A. All 19 questions in the assessment are derived from the material presented in this book and are designed to stimulate the often times avoided (and dreaded) organizational "soul" searching that is required for a true current state assessment.

The mapping serves its purpose as it sheds light on a major discrepancy between where the organization is today and the

> *No single answer is satisfactory for all organizations.*

stated desire to be at the Managed Innovation maturity level.

The mapping also shows what the organization must accomplish in each of the six traits to achieve a level four maturity. With this in mind, the organization can create a milestone-based plan that takes each yellow cell to the corresponding level four cell to achieve its desired innovation maturity.

A Common Sense Approach

A common sense approach to innovation begins with a solid understanding of the primary customer and that customer's needs. It recognizes that since organizations vary greatly in their cultures, purposes, people, processes, technologies, and metrics, no single answer is satisfactory for all organizations.

This means that any meaningful discussion about innovation must occur within a frame of reference that makes sense to the organization rather than purely for the sake of talking about innovation. An innovation maturity model is just one tool that an organization can leverage as they try to figure how innovative they currently are, how innovative they want to be, and how to get to where they would like to be.

Another useful tool to help guide the conversation about innovation is the Innovation Strategy Map shown in Figure 16. A strategy map is a diagram that is used to document the primary strategic goals being pursued by an organization.

The first strategy maps appeared in the early 1990s and were quickly adapted by Kaplan & Norton to help document the Balanced Scorecard. The standard strategy map has four perspectives – Learning and Growth, Internal Business Processes, Customer, and Financial, which are arranged from the bottom to top. The real value of the strategy map is its inherent simplicity and visual representation that enables a constructive discussion between leaders as to what the true "key" strategic objectives are and if necessary helps them perform a trade-off analysis to prioritize amongst competing objectives.

A common sense approach to innovation begins with a solid understanding of the primary customer and that customer's needs.

The Innovation Strategy Map realizes the same benefits for planning an innovation strategy that the standard strategy map provides for planning an overall business strategy. There is one difference though. The Innovation Strategy Map changes the order of the perspectives in the standard strategy map to Customer, Learning and Growth, Internal Business Process, and Financial (Figure 18).

This seemingly simple change has a profound implication – Innovation begins with the customer. It begins by understanding which of the following the customer values – service excellence, quality, price, intimacy/relationship, and leadership/brand – in which order, and how much, and then figuring out what the customer's pain points are in the "job" they are trying to get done using your product or service.

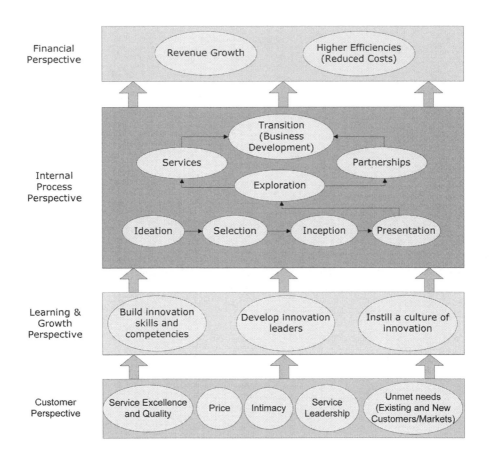

Figure 18: The Innovation Strategy Map changes the order of perspectives to ensure the primary focus remains on the customer.

This understanding is what drives the organizational skills, capabilities, and competencies you will need, which in turn directly impacts your business processes. If these three perspectives are handled properly, the financial perspective will follow naturally. Many innovations fail simply because they focus too much on the financial perspective rather than helping the customer get their job done. In fact, as we discussed in Chapter 10, an excessive focus on financial outcomes such as ROI is a primary reason why many potentially promising ideas never even make it past the ideation phase.

The Bottom Line

✓ The innovation maturity model provides an objective tool to assess where an organization currently is in its innovation maturity and provides guidance on creating a roadmap that can help align it with where it would like to be as an innovating organization.

✓ There is no good or bad, right or wrong maturity level. Each organization must decide itself what level makes sense for it.

✓ Advancing from one maturity level to the next is a journey that involves affecting all six traits in varying degrees. This journey and the time within which it is accomplished are unique to each organization.

Epilogue

Living and prospering in the Innovation Age, where innovation is neither an option nor a luxury but rather a way of life, requires organizational leaders to re-evaluate how they think about and approach innovation.

In his book, *The Innovator's Dilemma*, Christensen describes a theory about how large, outstanding firms often fail "by doing everything right" (Christensen, The Innovator's Dilemma: When New Technologies Cause Great Firms to Fall, 2000). It is a dilemma in which a company's successes and core capabilities can actually become obstacles in the face of changing markets and technologies. Such companies often face a catch-22 of maintaining their current customers, their relations in their value-network, and meeting the growth expectations of their shareholders without sacrificing near-term profits. The advent of the Innovation Age has only served to bring this dilemma to the forefront!

As we have explored throughout this book, continuous innovation that can drive sustainable competitive advantage is much broader than the disruptive "eureka" moments of innovation legends. Creating an organizational culture that embraces a philosophy of continuous innovation requires that leaders invest, nurture, and sustain an open and collaborative environment in which taking measured risks is encouraged and innovation is viewed as a long-term journey that goes "where no man has gone before."

May you live long and prosper in the Innovation Age!

Appendix A

Innovation Quotient Self-Assessment

This self-assessment will help you determine the innovation quotient for your organization. All 19 questions are derived from the material presented in this book. There is a quick reference "Answer Guide" at the end of this appendix that maps each question to the most relevant portions of the book where you can find more information.

Instructions

The instructions for completing this self-assessment are fairly simple:

1. Choose the most appropriate answer for each of the 19 questions. The questions are straight forward and there are no trick questions. Still, do not be surprised if many of these questions cause you to pause and do some organizational "soul" searching.
2. Calculate your organization's Innovation Quotient by adding up the points for each of the 19 answers. The points for each answer are indicated in the parentheses next to the answer.
3. The Innovation Quotient should be a number between -21 and 34. If it's not, this might be a good time to get your calculator☺.

4. Find out where your organization falls on the scale from "Needs Improvement" to "Excellent" using the table below:

Interpreting your organization's Innovation Quotient	
Needs Improvement	-21 to 11
Average	12 to 22
Good	23 to 28
Excellent	29 to 34

5. Review the quick reference "Answer Guide" to refresh your knowledge on how you can help improve your organization's Innovation Quotient. If you haven't already read the whole book once, I strongly recommend just starting from the beginning (Introduction) to receive the most benefit.
6. Maximize your Innovation Quotient by:
    a. Repeating this self-assessment at least once a year to check your progress and find "focus areas" on which to concentrate.
    b. Involving others from your senior leadership team in multiple individual assessments or a single joint assessment.
    c. Following up your assessment with working sessions with other senior leaders to brainstorm ways to improve your organization's score in identified focus areas. Or better yet, employ Principle 4 (Innovation Seeks to Be Free) by leveraging open innovation and crowdsourcing techniques to broaden your participation and ownership of the solution.
7. Leverage the insight gained from your organizational "soul" searching to plot and compare the "current state" of your organization's innovation maturity with its desired (future) state (see Chapter 11, Applying the Innovation Maturity Model). Analyzing the gaps can further assist in creating a roadmap that can guide your organization's innovation journey.

Questions

1. Does your organization identify innovation as a strategic mandate?
    - ○ Yes (+1)
    - ○ No (-1)

2. What is the primary purpose of innovation in your organization?
    - ○ Survival (-1)
    - ○ Organic growth (+1)
    - ○ Expanding the core with new products and services (+2)
    - ○ Sustain competitive advantage by actively seeking disruption (+3)

3. What drives innovation in your organization?
    - ○ Keeping up with competitors (-1)
    - ○ Customer feedback, surveys, and focus groups (+1)
    - ○ Employees and partners (+1)
    - ○ An understanding of the customer's "job" (+2)

4. Does your organization view each problem as an opportunity to innovate?
    - ○ Yes (+1)
    - ○ No (-1)

5. What is the level of risk tolerance in your organization?
    - ○ None (-1)
    - ○ Tepid (+1)
    - ○ Risk taking is encouraged (+2)
    - ○ Risks are actively sought out (+3)

6. Does your innovation strategy identify different innovation types for different categories of products or services based on the maturity of the market they serve or other factors?
    - ○ Yes (+1)
    - ○ No (-1)

7. Who is ultimately responsible for innovation?
    - ○ Individuals on their own time (-1)
    - ○ Specialized R&D teams (+1)
    - ○ Informal groups formed around ideas (+2)
    - ○ Top management as mandated by your innovation strategy (+3)

8. Who is responsible for implementing "innovative" ideas in your organization?
   - O No one (-2)
   - O R&D ideates and implements and then turns over to the field (-1)
   - O R&D comes up with the ideas and field personnel implement them (-1)
   - O A joint multi-disciplinary team consisting of subject experts and field personnel (+2)

9. Which individuals are valued higher in your organization?
   - O Highly specialized experts (+1)
   - O Professionals who are a few feet deep but a mile wide (+2)

10. How are ideas collected in your organization?
    - O No formal method (-2)
    - O Suggestion box (-1)
    - O An open and transparent ideas portal (+2)

11. How does your organization decide which ideas to select and move forward?
    - O ROI (-1)
    - O Gut feeling (+1)
    - O "Game changing" potential of the idea (+2)

12. Do you understand the lifecycle of how innovation progresses from idea to market transition in your organization?
    - O Yes (+1)
    - O No (-1)

13. Does your organization have a pipeline of ideas in various stages of development?
    - O Yes (+1)
    - O No (-1)

14. Does your workspace environment stimulate your mind?
    - O Yes (+1)
    - O No (-1)

15. Is your work environment conducive to collaboration either virtually or physically?
    O Yes (+1)
    O No (-1)

16. Does your organization clearly value efficiency over innovation?
    O Yes (-2)
    O No (+2)

17. Does your organization provide employees with dedicated time to innovate?
    O Yes (+2)
    O No (0)

18. Does your organization have clearly defined incentives tied to innovation?
    O Yes (+2)
    O No (-2)

19. How does your organization measure innovation?
    O No metrics (-2)
    O One-dimensional metrics such as ROI and R&D budget (-1)
    O Metrics based on idea generation and execution (+1)
    O Percent sales from new products and services (+2)

Quick Reference Answer Guide

Here is a quick mapping of each question with the relevant portion of the book. This is in no way a comprehensive mapping as many of the concepts are spread across several different areas. So, please only use this mapping as a starting point.

Question	Quick References
Does your organization identify innovation as a strategic mandate?	Chapter 7 (Articulating a clear Innovation Strategy), Chapter 11.
What is the primary purpose of innovation in your organization?	Chapter 1 (The Need for Continuous Innovation), Chapter11.
What drives innovation in your organization?	Chapter 1 (Customer centric paradox), Chapter 5.
Does your organization view each problem as an opportunity to innovate?	Chapter 4.
What is the level of risk tolerance in your organization?	Chapter 3.
Does your innovation strategy identify different innovation types for different categories of products or services based on the maturity of the market they serve or other factors?	Chapter 6.
Who is primarily responsible for innovation?	Chapter 7 (Gauging Organizational Commitment), Chapter 7 (Recognizing That Actions Speak Louder Than Words).
Who is responsible for implementing "innovative" ideas in your organization?	Chapter 2, Chapter 8 (Making Innovation a Team Sport).

Which individuals are valued higher in your organization?	Chapter 8.
How are ideas collected in your organization?	Chapter 5, Chapter 8 (Collecting ideas from Everyone and Everywhere), Chapter 10 (Ideation).
How does your organization decide which ideas to select and move forward?	Chapter 10 (Selection).
Do you understand the lifecycle of how innovation progresses from idea to market transition in your organization?	Chapter 10.
Does your organization have a pipeline of ideas in various stages of development?	Chapter 10.
Does your workspace environment stimulate your mind?	Chapter 8 (Rethinking Workspace Design).
Is your work environment conducive to collaboration either virtually or physically?	Chapter 8 (Rethinking Workspace Design), Chapter 8 (Harnessing the Community).
Does your organization clearly value efficiency over innovation?	Chapter 3, Chapter 9.
Does your organization provide employees with dedicated time to innovate?	Chapter 3.
Does your organization have clearly defined incentives tied to innovation?	Chapter 7 (Gauging Organizational Commitment), Chapter 7 (Recognizing That Actions Speak Louder Than Words).
How does your organization measure innovation?	Chapter 9.

Appendix B

Quick Notes

This appendix aggregates the Bottom Line sections from each chapter into one place for quick reference.

Chapter 1

- ✓ We have already entered the Innovation Age in which the new norm is continuous innovation. Innovation is not an option nor a luxury but the new way of life.

- ✓ Innovation is not about a faster horse; it is about really understanding what the customer's needs are. At the same time, beware of the customer centric paradox.

- ✓ Innovation applies to all – whether you are in the private sector, the public sector, or a not-for-profit organization.

Chapter 2

- ✓ The hardest part of innovation is not coming up with good ideas.

- ✓ No matter how good an idea is, it is just an abstraction. To be useful an idea must be implemented.

- ✓ Mediocre ideas can lead to successful innovation. The best ideas don't always win.

Chapter 3

- ✓ The road to successful innovation is paved with failures.
- ✓ Successful innovations are not necessarily the result of gifted people having groundbreaking epiphanies.
- ✓ Organizations are typically designed for efficiencies not innovation.

Chapter 4

- ✓ Innovators never shy away from challenging the status quo with questions such as "what if," "why," and "why not."
- ✓ Constraints provide a fertile ground for innovation. Both existing constraints as well as imposed constraints can spur innovation.
- ✓ Innovation in one field is often the result of adopting "common" ideas from another field.

Chapter 5

- ✓ Innovation thrives in environments that encourage collaboration, participation, and open communication.
- ✓ Many successful innovations are the result of ideas that originated outside the organization.
- ✓ Organizations need to cultivate a culture in which innovation is everyone's responsibility not just of the chosen few in R&D labs.

Chapter 6

- ✓ Innovation is not a one-size-fits-all proposition.
- ✓ Innovation is not just limited to end user products and services,; innovation can also take the form of business model changes and internal or customer facing process improvements
- ✓ Regardless of the type of innovation, the ultimate focus must be on providing value and meeting currently unmet needs of your customers.

Chapter 7

- ✓ True innovation requires organizational commitment to a culture shift away from just emphasizing efficiencies and near-term results.

- ✓ Innovation cannot be an afterthought. It must be well thought out and articulated with a corporate level innovation strategy.

- ✓ Senior leaders are as responsible – if not more – for ensuring real innovation occurs by showing it in their actions and not just their words.

Chapter 8

- ✓ Innovative organizations attract other innovators by providing an environment that promotes the free exchange and confluence of ideas from different areas.

- ✓ Innovative ideas can come from anyone, anywhere, and anytime.

- ✓ Innovation thrives when everyone from across the company is involved in it from the very beginning. Conversely, innovation rarely succeeds in a "throw it over the wall" type environment.

Chapter 9

- ✓ Keep it simple by focusing on metrics that make sense to your environment.

- ✓ There are no magic metrics or silver bullets. The best approach is to use a balanced set of metrics that cover the entire innovation lifecycle.

- ✓ Imposing rigid processes with the goal of measuring everything could have an adverse effect of stifling your innovation initiatives.

Chapter 10

- ✓ Innovation thrives in an environment that encourages experimentation. Make sure your innovation lifecycle reflects this as well.

- ✓ An effective innovation lifecycle ensures that the most valuable ideas continue to move forward from initial concept to final production in a systematic and orderly manner.

- ✓ Recognize the difference between outputs and outcomes.

Chapter 11

- ✓ The innovation maturity model provides an objective tool to assess where an organization currently is in its innovation maturity and provides guidance on creating a roadmap that can help align it with where it would like to be as an innovating organization.

- ✓ There is no good or bad, right or wrong maturity level. Each organization must decide itself what level makes sense for it.

- ✓ Advancing from one maturity level to the next is a journey that involves affecting all six traits in varying degrees. This journey and the time within which it is accomplished are unique to each organization.

Bibliography

"iamnotjamesh". (2011, February). *THIN IS IN. GET THAT STRAIGHT DELL.* Retrieved from Idea Storm.

Vision Statement: The $300 House. (2011). Retrieved from http://hbr.org/2011/10/the-300-house/ar/pr

Ante, S. (2008). Sprint's Wake-Up Call. *Bloomberg Businessweek.*

Arthur, C. (2011). Samsung battle with Apple in tablets and smartphones enters new legal stage. *The Guardian.*

Atkinson, R., & Andes, S. (2011). The Atlantic Century II: Benchmarking EU & U.S. Innovation and Competitiveness. *Information Technology and Innovation Foundation.*

Berkun, S. (2007). *The Myths of Innovation.* O'Reilly Media.

Brass, D. (2010). Microsoft's Creative Destruction . *The New York Times.*

Brown, T., & Ulijn, J. (2004). *Innovation, Entrepreneurship and Culture: The Interaction Between Technology, Progress and Economic Growth.* Edward Elgar Pub .

Burke, B., & Mesaglio, M. (2010). *Case Study: Innovation Squared: The Department for Work and Pensions Turns Innovation Into a Game.* Gartner.

Carlson, C. (2011). Taco Bell, KFC, Pizza Hut workers worldwide sharing ideas online. *FierceCIO*.

Chakravorty, B. (2010). Finding Competitive Advantage in Adversity. *Harvard Business Review*.

Chesbrough, H. (2003). *Open Innovation: The New Imperative for Creating and Profiting from Technology*. Harvard Business Press.

Christensen, C. M. (2000). *The Innovator's Dilemma: When New Technologies Cause Great Firms to Fall*. Highbridge Company.

Christensen, C. M. (2003). *The Innovator's Solution: Creating and Sustaining Successful Growth*. Harvard Business Press.

Christensen, C. M. (2010). *Innovation Killers: How Financial Tools Destroy Your Capacity to Do New Things* . Harvard Business Press.

Copulsky, J., & Hutt., K. (2006). Gambling with the House's Money: The Randomness of Corporate Innovation.

Countries of the Third World - Nations Online Project. (n.d.). Retrieved from http://www.nationsonline.org/oneworld/third_world.htm

Darwin, C. (1859). *On the Origin of Species*. John Murray.

Dilbert.com. (2004, February 16, 17). *Dilbert*. Retrieved from http://dilbert.com/strips/comic/2004-02-16/, http://dilbert.com/strips/comic/2004-02-17/

Drucker, P. (1993). *Innovation and Entrepreneurship*. Collins.

Dyer, J., Gregersen, H., & Christensen, C. M. (2011). *The Innovator's DNA: Mastering the Five Skills of Disruptive Innovators*. Harvard Business Press.

Evans, H., Buckland, G., & Lefer, D. (2004). *They Made America: From the Steam Engine to the Search Engine: Two Centuries of Innovators* . Little, Brown and Company.

Evans, M. (n.d.). *Power of Crowdsourcing*. Retrieved from http://www.exinfm.com/board/crowdsourcing.htm

Fingar, P. (2006). *Extreme Competition: Innovation And the Great 21st Century Business Reformation*. Meghan Kiffer Pr.

Forden, S., & Womack, B. (2011). Google Settles FTC Privacy Charges on 'Buzz' Social Network. *Bloomberg Businessweek*.

Gates, B. (2001). Gates Showcases Tablet PC, Xbox at COMDEX; Says New "Digital Decade" Technologies Will Transform How We Live. *Microsoft News Center*.

Gaudin, S. (2011). Social tools help drug maker fix supply chain. *Computerworld*.

Google Investor Relations. (2011). *Google Announces First Quarter 2011 Results* . Retrieved from http://investor.google.com/earnings/2011/Q1_google_earnings.ht ml

Govindarajan, V., & Trimble, C. (2010). *The Other Side of Innovation*. Harvard Business Press.

Govindrajan, V. (2006, March). *Strategy as Transformation*. Retrieved from Vijay Govidrajan's Blog: http://www.vijaygovindarajan.com/2006/03/strategy_as_transforma tion.htm

Govindrajan, V. (2010, August). *The $300 House: A Hands-On Lab for Reverse Innovation?* Retrieved from http://blogs.hbr.org/govindarajan/2010/08/the-300-house-a-hands-on-lab-f.html

Gruley, B., & Edwards, C. (2011, November). What is Sony Now? *Bloomberg Businessweek*.

Gustin, S. (2011). Google Says Microsoft's Latest Android Lawsuit Threatens Innovation. *Wired Magazine*.

Hampton, A. (2011). Best in SF government social media. *sf.govfresh*.

Hindo, B. (2007). At 3M, A Struggle Between Efficiency And Creativity . *Bloomberg Businessweek*.

Howe, J. (2006). The Rise of Crowdsourcing. *Wired Magazine*.

Hunter, R., & Westerman, G. (2009). *Real Business of IT: How CIOs Create and Communicate Value* . Harvard Business Press.

Jacobs, J. (1970). *The Economy of Cities*. Vintage .

Jana, R. (2009). How the Government Can Do Good with Less. *Bloomberg BusinessWeek*.

Jaruzelski, B., & Dehoff, K. (2010). The Global Innovation 1000. *Strategy + Business*.

Jobs, S. (2008). Steve Jobs speaks out. (B. Morris, Interviewer) CNN Money.

Johnson, S. (2010). *Where Good Ideas Come From: The Natural History of Innovation*. Riverhead Hardcover.

Kotter, J. P. (2010). *Buy-In: Saving Your Good Idea from Getting Shot Down* . Harvard Business Press.

Krazit, T. (2010). Oracle sues Google over Android and Java. *CNet News*.

Krishnan, M., & Prahalad, C. (2008). *The New Age of Innovation: Driving Cocreated Value through Global Networks*. McGraw-Hill.

Leucke, R., & Katz, R. (2003). *Managing Creativity and Innovation*. Harvard Business Review.

MergeGlobal. (2006). *General Aviation's Contribution to the U.S. Economy*. Retrieved from http://www.ok.gov/OAC/documents/General%20Aviation%20Co ntribution%20to%20the%20US%20Economy%20(GAMA).pdf

Miller, J. (2011). OMB releases details of cloud-first policy for agencies. *Federal News Radio*.

Moore, G. (2005). *Dealing with Darwin: How Great Companies Innovate at Every Phase of Their Evolution.* Portfolio Hardcover.

Nobelprize.org. (n.d.). *Linus Pauling - Biography.* Retrieved from http://www.nobelprize.org/nobel_prizes/peace/laureates/1962/pauling-bio.html

Phillips, T. (2011). Mark Zuckerberg confirms he's joined Google+, wonders why that's weird. *Metro.*

Pink, D. (2005). *A Whole New Mind.* Riverhead .

Richardson, A. (2010). *Innovation X: Why a Company's Toughest Problems Are Its Greatest Advantage.* Jossey-Bass.

Salter, C. (2008). Marissa Mayer's 9 Principles of Innovation. *Fast Company.*

Siklos, R. (2009). Information wants to be free ... and expensive. *CNN Money.*

Snopes.com. (n.d.). *New Coke Origins.* Retrieved from http://www.snopes.com/cokelore/newcoke.asp

Software Engineering Institute. (n.d.). *CMMI Overview.* Retrieved from http://www.sei.cmu.edu/cmmi/

Solar Bottle Bulb. (n.d.). Retrieved from http://isanglitrongliwanag.org/

The Economist. (2009). The revolution that wasn't. *The Economist.*

The Super Cars. (2011). *Most Expensive Cars In The World: Top 10 List 2011-2012.* Retrieved from http://www.thesupercars.org/top-cars/most-expensive-cars-in-the-world-top-10-list/

The White House. (2009). *Open Government Directive.* Retrieved from whitehouse.gov: http://www.whitehouse.gov/open/documents/open-government-directive

The White House. (2011). *Remarks by the President in State of Union Address.* Retrieved from The White House: http://www.whitehouse.gov/the-press-office/2011/01/25/remarks-president-state-union-address

Vaitheeswaran, V., & Carson, I. (2007). *The Age of Mass Innovation.* Economist.

Vance, A. (2011, September 1). When Patents Attack: Could Facebook Be Next? *Bloomberg Businessweek.*

Wagner, A. (2011). Google Buys Motorola: The Patent Wars Ramp Up. *The Huffington Post.*

Wallop, H. (2011). Japan earthquake: how Twitter and Facebook helped. *The Telegraph.*

Wikipedia. (n.d.). *Ideation (Idea Generation).* Retrieved from http://en.wikipedia.org/wiki/Ideation_(idea_generation)

Index

Living in the Innovation Age

About the Author

Tarak Modi is the Vice President and Chief Technology Officer at CALIBRE Systems, Inc., an employee-owned management and technology services company, where he leads the effort in leveraging technology through the innovative use of IT to create and sustain long-term competitive advantage. A champion of innovation, he is an industry thought leader in IT transformation and modernization technology such as enterprise architecture, Service Oriented Architecture, and Cloud Computing. A prolific author with excellent communication skills, Tarak has also co-authored *Professional Java Web Services* (Wrox Press, 2001) and published over 80 articles that showcase his broad experience, keen business acumen, and deep technical knowledge. Find out more about Tarak at his professional website, TekNirvana.com.

Made in the USA
Charleston, SC
03 December 2012